SOWS' EARS
AND SILK PURSES

SOWS' EARS AND SILK PURSES

Ann Drysdale

Routledge & Kegan Paul
London, Boston, Melbourne and Henley

First published in 1984
by Routledge & Kegan Paul plc

39 Store Street, London WC1E 7DD, England

9 Park Street, Boston, Mass. 02108, USA

464 St Kilda Road, Melbourne,
Victoria 3004, Australia and

Broadway House, Newtown Road,
Henley-on-Thames, Oxon RG9 1EN, England

Set in 11/13 Stempel Garamond by
Inforum Ltd, Portsmouth
and printed in Great Britain by
Billings Ltd, Worcester

Library of Congress Cataloging in Publication Data

Drysdale, Ann.
Sows' ears and silk purses.
Sequel to: Faint heart never kissed a pig.
Bibliography: p.
1. Farm life—England—North Yorkshire. 2. Drysdale,
Ann. 3. North Yorkshire—Social life and customs.
I. Title.
S522.G7D793   1984   942.8'10858'0924   83-21322

ISBN 0-7100-9912-6

Contents

Hagg House (Adrian Herbert)

Sows' Ears

The first time my elder son came home from boarding school for the weekend, he came and went by train.

Another step towards growing up, towards independence. At his age I had coped happily with trains, London termini, great streams of crawling buses and even the Tube, which I took so much for granted and in which my children do not quite believe. Why, then, do I wonder at the lad's capability? Perhaps because I have a worry that by bringing them up in the wilderness I am depriving them of urbanity's benefits. More likely that I regret, slightly, the slipping-away of his dependence.

I saw him off on the platform of Northallerton station, which is not, by anyone's standards, the hub of British Rail, but I was still depressed by the overwhelming aura of good-bye, the echoing of footsteps in the quiet pauses between the roar of highspeed, non-stop trains, and I felt dusty, grey and miserable as I went back to the barrier to return the platform ticket to the clerk.

I remembered my arrival in Yorkshire, years ago, which was accomplished, for want of a better way, by train.

It was by way of a last throw of the dice, a final effort at finding somewhere to live that I could afford, that I could hang on to while I tried to put back together a family that seemed, on reflection, to be damaged beyond repair.

Friends had a cottage near York and the adjacent property was to let. They were putting in a good word and I was going down there to be ready to move in.

At the time I was staying with my in-laws in Edinburgh, and they were very worried about the step I was taking, but they applauded my bravery. I was too giddy at the shock of having made such a decision to acknowledge their applause, but I felt suddenly taller, and my stature grew apace as the plans progressed. I booked the seats for York.

The day before we were to leave, the letter came. My friends had discovered that the cottage we had hoped for was no longer to let, but that they would go on looking. I decided to pretend that the letter had never arrived, and tore it into tiny pieces which I screwed up and dropped into the lavatory.

Truth will out, they say, but you can have it on my authority that it will not down. Twice I flushed the system, but still the bits spun giddily round in the bowl and as I waited for the cistern to fill, my mother-in-law loomed against the frosted glass and asked if I had had another accident with those dreadful disposable nappies. I decided against a third try, skimmed the bits off the surface and posted them out through the window. We were two floors up in a tenement block, and the bits fell soundlessly to the 'back green'. They probably ended up mixed with sharp sand to relieve someone's pot-bound geranium or got scooped up with a dessert-spoon in someone's after-dusk trip to refill the cat's sanitary tray. All I cared then was that my relatives-by-marriage should not discover that their fears about their English daughter's sanity were wholly grounded.

The following day we went by taxi to the station. I refused to let my face drop its farewell-mother smile until she and my sister-in-law whizzed backwards into obscurity and only then did I take stock.

There seemed rather a lot of stock to take. Two babies,

riding rather high in their carrycots because of all necessities stowed under their mattresses. A pram full of less immediate but bulkier necessities, stowed in the guard's van and how in hell was I to get it out. And Andrew, whose cheery faith in my knowledge of what was best made my mouth feel like a neglected fireplace and filled my throat with marbles. Beside him sat Jack, the aged bear who had seen him through so many crises, and his button eyes turned to heaven and his luggage label, brazenly printed with my friends' address, made him look like a furry evacuee. Poor displaced ursine.

I polished up the corners of my smile and set about making enough strong acquaintances to lift all my accoutrements off the train at York.

York station is like any other. Long and thin, with that tunnellish one-way-traffic feeling that sums up most adult nightmares. Everything was piled on the platform and it only needed a couple of comic bailiffs to complete the air of pantomime. My friends had come for me and we were sitting in the cafeteria faced with cups of British Rail tea. People often complain about the quality of the beverage when served in these circumstances but they fail to take into account that the very sameness of it all over the country makes a rock for the travel-weary in strange places and does more to bring the far corners nearer together than the trains themselves.

I could see my cup sitting on the table. I couldn't drink it because I had a baby in each arm, but there was comfort in the thick, purple look of it, and the horse-piss smell cried welcome louder than my waiting friends. Not that I blamed them for their reserve. I did have an awesome array of impedimenta. One of them took Nancy from me and I took my first sip of a comfort so tangible that I felt myself on the verge of tears, like the effect of a kind word on a lonely child at a new school. I provoked my friends to witticism to dispel the mood, but it was reflected back from Andrew's pale little

3

face and from the orange-squash tear that ran down Jack's nose where he had spilled his drink.

But all that was a long time ago and by the time Andrew's train was a rumble in the distance, I was myself again, with a roof over my head, coping somehow, seeing my elder son off to Grammar School. But I had travelled a long way during the ten minutes it took me to see him off and so much of what I dreamed of then had become a reality that we were all of us beginning to take it for granted.

In the first of these books I began to explain how we came to live at Hagg House Farm in the middle of the North Yorkshire Moors.

It is far harder to explain, even to myself, how I made it into a home and a small business and picked up the threads of a journalistic career I thought I had thrown away. But I took my sow's ear and set out to make a silk purse of it; just how successful I have been I am still too close to see clearly. In this book I hope to try.

Imagine a bird so ugly that a creator of movie monsters would have been proud to have conceived it. A bulbous body clad in sombre houndstooth check with a spindling neck upon which is balanced a head of the most unenviable aspect. A face chalk-white and wrinkled dwindling to a cruel beak, all dominated by a horny excrescence like a policeman's helmet and flanked by trembling scarlet wattles that give the bird an air of irascibility that is underlined by its erratic, pickety progress and constant disgruntled muttering. All the design features of the turkey without his imposing appearance and any pretension to dignity denied by the presence, on either side of the head, of two dingy earholes which sprout a few ginger whiskers and whose depths, on inspection, appear to contain as unsavoury an accumulation of debris as those of the archetypal schoolboy and which the beastly bird empties from time to time with the longest toes of its skinny feet. And there you have the guinea-fowl.

When the Lord, in His wisdom, designed the guinea-fowl, He built into it some remarkable refinements, but these seem to have been carried so much to extremes that they must have been intended as divine experiments; dummy runs, as it were, for the less exaggerated wildfowl. The pheasant and the partridge must surely have been developed as utilitarian spin-offs from that original flight of omnipotent fancy.

Dodo, the first guinea-fowl I had ever owned, worried me deeply with her desperate loneliness which I was powerless to alleviate until I ascertained her sex. Finally, acting on doubtful information and inspired impulse, I purchased Archie from a friend. The resultant clutches of eggs, regarded by my neighbours as the inevitable outcome of the enterprise, were none the less, for me, a delightful surprise, as I remained unconvinced, even to the last, that any creature, even another guinea-fowl, could ever fancy anything as blatantly unlovely as my poor Dodo.

I ended my first book with the story of the coming-together of the pair as a fairly typical example of the way things began for us here, after my husband left and I made up my mind to stay and make a life for myself and the children – Andrew and the twins Nancy and Robert – in what I had begun to look on as a very special place. I saw the life of the hill farmer as something true and honest in a world that was becoming daily more distasteful to me. I saw the innocent coming-together of the two extraordinary birds as a symbol of the optimism that was all I had to carry me on towards the establishment of the small farm I longed to make from the unlikely assortment of creatures I had accumulated. But every story has a continuation; nothing stops to wait for us and as each beginning ends, so the end is beginning even as the tale unfolds.

When Dodo went broody, all through a sizzling drought, she sat in state in a clump of wilting brackens behind the house, her perfect camouflage ruined by the ceaseless sentry-go of the ambulant Archie. I was told that the dry weather, curse as it was to crops and grassland, would favour her chicks when they hatched, and I was regaled with stories of whole broods of such youngsters carried away with pneumonia after a particularly heavy dew.

This comforted me all through their incubation. On the day they finally hatched, the weather broke in icy torrents and my worries began.

Her first-hatched had already died quietly in a jury-rigged incubator, chilled by his mother's momentary absence, and I realised that the rest of the brood would have a better chance of survival if I were to transfer them to a coop in the yard, so I set one up, complete with wire run, drownproof water container and full-length roof. All that remained was to catch Dodo and her downy dozen and put them in it. All!

A broody hen, when approached, fluffs herself up, adopts a threatening expression, and summons her babies under the protection of her spread wings. She is not difficult to catch, and the chicks are usually scooped up in an apronful of fuzz and feet, the whole issue being transported to a place of safety with little effort.

The guinea-fowl, on the other hand, plays the game-bird and rises to her tiptoes, with stretched neck, uttering the clarion call 'Scatter!' And scatter they do, in all directions at a speed almost unbelievable in creatures only hours old. Several attempts at catching Dodo unawares proved the futility of any such plan of campaign and ended in frantic efforts to locate whistling nestlings, clapped down in the long grass and all but invisible.

Finally I caught them by superior strategy. A trail of chick crumbs led into the wire run and ended in a great heap of guinea-goodies at the far end. While they stuffed themselves I crept up and cut off their escape with the wooden coop. I had them.

Two days later an adventurous chick crept out through a hole dibbled by the ducks under the wire and died, chilled, in the early hours. There were now 11.

Archie's vigil continued. From sunrise till sunset he was never out of sight of his wife and children. At night he roosted on the corner of the goat pen, and he was first up every morning, beating even the bantam cock in the first flutter to the ground.

He was justly proud of his offspring. Seven stripey ones, two white ones and two an unlikely shade of faded denim blue, and I watched them grow, absorbing chick crumbs by the bucketful while their feathers sprouted. The stripey ones became navy blue with white houndstooth check, like their parents, the denims kept their pretty blue and gained white polka dots, but the white stayed white, except where the mud splashed up, and their eyes were sapphire blue.

I kept them penned up longer than I should have done through sheer cowardice. It was only when the weather brightened and the warmth of the sun drew forth from the little run a smell that I could not quite place that I thought of liberating them, and when the elusive smell finally clicked as the echo of a broiler house I had once walked through, I kicked the coop aside and crossed my fingers.

Out came the chicks, straight to the pond for a drink, and into the murky depths fell the smallest white one. I fished him out, dried him in the oven, and set him going again like a clockwork toy. My year's experience had taught me to tell the difference between feminine creaks and masculine whistles, and I named him Jethro.

Perhaps it was giving him a name that did it, perhaps it was the attention he merited as the smallest chick, but he seemed always to be in the front line of any trouble. One morning he stayed in the sleeping-pile when all the others had set forth to forage, shivering and puffed up, with his head huddled on to his shoulders like a tiny vulture with Spanish tummy. I put him in the oven again, and mused on the paradox these birds presented.

The adults of the species are among the hardiest of domestic fowl, sleeping outside in all but the wildest weather and seemingly impervious to rain and sleet, while the young are notoriously delicate, huddling in heaps at the foot of their parents' roosting place like a group of cockney children playing Jump-Jimmy-Knacker in an alley, the only difference being that the littlest ones always seemed to be left on the top of the pile and a cold wet night would wipe them out were it not for human interference in the shape of welly-booted women who scoop them up in handfuls and hurl them into henhuts to preserve them from the worst ravages of the elements.

A few nights later, however, I had returned late from Swainby sheep sale and the chicks must have been as wet as I was even before I put them under cover, and thus Jethro ended up in the oven yet again, together with two siblings.

For the next couple of days he stayed in the house; one of the other two had died, one had been returned to the flock as cured and little Jethro crept round the sitting-room like a carpet-slippered long stay patient in a geriatric ward, hunching in corners while I sought him, expecting to find a stiff little corpse on the quarry tiles every time I came into the room. But he lived.

One morning I counted the flock as they rolled up for breakfast and there were still ten. I counted them again after I had exercised the dog, and there were nine. Jethro was missing and I feared a violent end.

The poor mite was so peaky and vulnerable, like the baby in the old song – the one that fell down the plug-hole – he was so skinny and thin he was almost bound to fall by the wayside. All the same I mourned him and searched half-heartedly for evidence.

Failing to find a sad little pile of feathers in any of the obvious places I went back into the house and there, sitting on the couch, encircled by drooling cats, was Jethro, whistling out a complicated tale like a spindly Scheherezade until rescue came.

I caught him up, rejoicing, and put him outside the door.

He shuffled to the edge of the step. His little bald head shone pink in the watery sunshine and his orange feet plopped one before the other in his unhurried search for the rest of his family.

And for some silly reason I laughed till the corners of my mouth felt stretched and my sides felt quite sore.

In those early days the collecting of creatures was like a happy game of chance. One by one they found their way to us, these happy discoveries, each bringing their own tests and demands, challenging what little skill I could bring to bear upon any situation which confronted me. Snuff the black sheep, Magnus the Shetland pony, a succession of goats – Emily, Bobo, Laura and Googie – all these arrived, many unheralded and most unsolicited. Others were scrimped and saved and greatly longed for like Rosalie Pig and our first Swaledale sheep.

Many of them are still with us, but others have long since gone, leaving only pictures dimly remembered and sounds half recalled, like our first duck, Onion, and our first drake, Sage. I can hear him still.

A mechanical sort of sound, rather like the sound of a wooden spoon being drawn across a nutmeg grater, rhythmic and insistent – grrrrrit, grrrrit. That was Sage, the drake, muttering his lonely threnody under the window, where he sat, night after night, keeping his vigil over the rickety little hen-coop where Onion, his beloved mate and erstwhile constant companion, had other fish to fry. If you see what I mean.

There were nine blue eggs in that hencoop and sprawled above them sat Onion, head under her wing, fixing passers-by with a beady stare from the one shoe-button eye that peeped constantly. Round about that time of the morning, before the rest of the poultry had ventured forth, she would lift herself gingerly from her clutch and back out of the coop, covering the eggs carefully with the snowy down she provided herself so that they were completely hidden from prying eyes. When she had waddled a safe distance from the nest, she let out her raucous wark-wark, like an over-enthusiastic farmyard impersonator at a pub talent night.

Sage would step towards her, radiating joy and pride, and bob his head in greeting. She stretched her neck, bending her head low, and together they trotted to the pond.

As they passed the kitchen door, I usually tossed out any accumulated scraps, so that I could have the pleasure of watching Sage behave like an old-world feathered gentle-man, indicating the choice pieces and even contriving to look genuinely happy as she bolted and gobbled everything I had to offer. Sage would flop about from scrap to scrap, pointing out goodies, even turning them for her with his beak, but not one morsel did he take for himself.

Then, together, they would go to the pond for a swim. No more frenzied early-morning lovemaking – now they would swim ceremonially round and round; Onion rising up in the water, splashing herself and preening busily; Sage watching possessively until she had finished her toilet, then escorting her back to the nest, and standing guard while she uncovered the eggs and settled her soaked breast-feathers comfortably on her knobby charges. Now I under-stood why duck eggs hatched under a hen have to be wetted surreptitiously from time to time. These blue dependants of dear Sage and Onion spent all their time in a damp and greasy fug generated by their wet and steamy mother, quite different from the fluffy warmth provided by the little white bantam who sat with equal determination on top of the straw bales in the loosebox.

When Onion was safely established once more on her clutch, Sage would walk sedately back to the yard, mutter-ing. Then, when he deemed himself safely out of sight and earshot of his beloved, he adopted a jaunty swagger as he returned alone to the pond. Now he indulged himself in a mad ten minutes, whirling, diving, standing on his tail and challenging all-comers, just as he used to do when he was showing off to his mate. Now, however, only the bald patch at the back of her head bore witness to their happy debauchery, that being the place where he used to hold on. Then he would come back to the kitchen door and I would find him a treat. I was very fond of Sage.

In a newspaper article, I described the mating procedure of Sage and Onion, and was told by an acquaintance that it was amusing – that it had the makings of a 'sexy article'. I thought about that a lot afterwards. I would like to think I had conveyed as successfully the simple, day-to-day affection; the wholehearted living of each and every moment of their ungainly duckitude.

There was only one cloud on the horizon as I waited for Onion to hatch out her brood.

I had been told that ducks did not make good mothers. That she was likely, should her young ones hatch, to gallop them round the meadows till they died of exhaustion, to float them round the pond like bath-ducks till they drowned, or even to neglect them utterly. It was pointed out in tones of quiet reasonableness that if I were to take her eggs, to 'banish' her from her nest, she would soon return to laying her daily egg for my own use. But they wouldn't have tasted the same.

These people who had lived all their lives among livestock, knew a great deal more about the workings of ducks than I did. I could not fathom why, if hens make such a better job of hatching the eggs, the Lord in His wisdom didn't make the hen lay duck eggs in the first place. I believed my friends to be right, and that Onion would make a hopeless mess of motherhood; countless people would tell me that they told me so. But still I defended to the last ditch her right to try.

I had my reasons. I am not as deaf or thick-skinned as my critics have been led to believe.

My own children were grubby and uncouth. Their language was sometimes questionable and their shoes seldom shone. It was occasionally hinted that they had more independence than was good for them. But I gave them what gifts I had to offer in my own way. No children were more dearly loved. My mother-in-law, I know, saw every hint of conformity with general standards as triumph of heredity over environment, and now and again I questioned my own criteria.

But I had quite made up my mind that if poor Onion could get a fraction of the joy that I had found in the bringing up of her young before her stupidity destroyed them utterly, she should have it.

There was a chance, after all, that we might both confound our detractors yet!

The Founding of the Flock

In those early days it was all fun. I brought up my scruffy children and tended my animal waifs and strays. My nearest neighbour, Jim, didn't object when they trespassed now and then on his grassland and I truly believed I had found the never-never land where I could play at farming forever and none of us need grow up unless we wanted to.

It is at times amusing to recollect that my earliest efforts to find a place for myself in this community nearly foundered for ever on communication difficulty.

A lift to a whist drive from a local resident seemed like a spell in purgatory as he made polite but totally unintelligible conversation, while I sat gripping the seat, trying to look listening and avoid saying yes or no, just in case. As a matter of record he proved a perfect gentleman.

Since then, my mastery of the local language has progressed to such an extent that not only can I understand it and to a degree, converse in it, but I have even contributed some words of my own which have passed into common usage.

Weeble (weak and feeble) was the name I gave to one of my first orphan lambs, an incredibly tiny wether, whose grim-faced tenacity to life became a legend in the dale and his name crops up in a variety of circumstances.

'That's a bit of a weeble', said a hill shepherd at clipping time, indicating an undeniably unpromising lamb which stood, all four feet on a threepenny bit, head drooping and back arched in an attitude of pure weebishness.

Thus, when I announced one spring, years ago that I had found a weeble on the road, everyone knew what it was; the only question outstanding was whose it might be. On a bitter, drizzling day I was walking along the road over the moor, when I saw, wedged upside-down between a stone wall and a wire fence, what appeared to be a dead sheep.

Investigation proved it to be a tiny female lamb, long weaned, which had been hit by a passing motorist and flung aside for dead. On setting her right-side-up, she raised her head, stared round at her hind leg, which was gashed to the bone, and groaned piteously. I got her on her feet, where-upon she passed a large amount of wind before collapsing once more among the ragwort.

I could recognise no mark of ownership, but she smelt of fresh dip and a blob of paint on her stubby horn suggested that she had been recently handled. But she was chilled, hurt and exhausted, so I took her home, dripping blood from her injured leg and passing wind intermittently as her innards slowly recovered from her upside-down posture.

An hour later, her leg cleaned and dressed and her diges-tive system primed with a basket of bramble leaves, I turned her loose in my tiny paddock. Like a woolly clockwork toy, she hobbled and munched with every evidence of recovery. A few telephone calls placed her as the lost property of a large farm nearby, but it was night and I had her back with me in the house to check her leg when I finally summoned the courage to ring her owner.

I knew him only by sight, a huge bluff man. I imagined him grinning as I explained what had happened and the waif herself chewed composedly under the china cabinet as I hinted that perhaps he might sell her to me. He roared with laughter, then fell silent.

Finally he said, with great solemnity, 'Well, Missus, what

I think is this – if it lives, it lives; if it dies, it dies. Either way, it's thy bugger and I've nowt to do with it.' Two little eyes like sucked brandy-balls watched me as I reached down the red dye and applied my own mark to her little hunched back.

I bore with equanimity the hoots of laughter from my friends, the good natured jokes about miniature sheep. I set about the task of putting some flesh on the tiny frame. I began with a few flakes of maize in the hollow of a house-brick. I sawed the legs off the hayrack so that she could reach it. Her bright eyes and skipping gait bespoke fitness, but she remained decidedly tiny.

In January her former owner died suddenly and the dale was the poorer for his passing. In a moment of quiet thought, I sat with the little one and as I stroked her rabbit head I noticed that at last the tiny stubs had begun to grow out into the curved horns of her breed. She had turned the corner. I decided to try and keep her, rather than sell her at the autumn sales with the rest.

In the spring, when it was time for the near-yearlings, now referred to as hoggs, to go out to the moor, I dipped her, dosed her against worms, re-applied the marks on her back and made my personal burn-mark on her horns as I had watched and helped the established moor shepherds do. Then I said goodbye and set her free.

She still seemed so undersized and vulnerable and I was secretly glad each time I walked along the moor bottom and saw her still lingering there, still answering my call, but I knew that her heritage was high up among the heather and I steeled myself to stay away for a whole week. When I went again she was gone.

At clipping time I eagerly scanned each gather. She came in among a bunch of youngsters from the far perimeter of the stray. A gawky young stranger, spindly from a summer's spurt of growth, she stood as tall as her companions and when I clipped her I felt a strength, a wildness in her that excited me. The brilliant eyes held a hint of recognition, but I dosed and remarked her coolly and turned her back once more to forage among her true kind.

That was the first ewe I ever turned out to run on the great moor that started from the side of the road above our house and stretched for mile upon mile stark and inhospitable to anything but the hardiest sheep and the grouse that giggled over their secrets in little private hollows.

She ran among Jim's sheep at tupping time and was heavy in lamb by the middle of March. On St Patrick's day I spied her looking faraway and sad, not eating hay with the rest. The next day she had lain down in a little hollow and would not move.

I carried her home and sought advice. I tried the few remedies I knew, and two days later she was dead. I dug a grave for her under the telegraph pole beside the house. It was a big dream to bury in such a small hole.

A bit of land and a few sheep is a very small thing to wish for, and yet at one time it seemed about as possible as taking over the whole of Yorkshire. I tried to feel defiance rather than misery when my early ventures with pet lambs became the subject of rivalry and competition that made failure more comfortable than success. So, when my first and only Swaledale sheep died while carrying that first longed-for lamb, I hardly felt able to share my unhappiness, since I had not been able to acknowledge her existence openly in the first place. I walked up the rigg to the ruckle, a stone landmark on the moor above the house, and wept miserably for the start I thought I had made that had turned into a pathetic little ending. Who was I, anyway, to attempt to keep sheep, when I had no real land of my own for them to run on. Better, perhaps, if I went back to the city, got a job and kept the children in what most people would have called a proper manner.

I imagined myself back in London, sitting in an office, trying to explain to the person I used to be just what it was I had found; just what it was I had lost. I sang to myself the song that first came into my mind – Scarborough Fair. How would I ever be able to hear it again without aching for this wild country that had no room in its cold heart for me. I could not farm on half an acre of tarmac and I thought miserably of the words of the song – 'tell him to find me an acre of land/between the salt water and the sea strand' – and told myself that with this insoluble riddle as my talisman I should give up and admit defeat.

I picked up a stone and threw it at the ruckle in a fresh storm of self-pity. It split neatly in half and embedded in the piece that rolled back to my feet was the fossil of a sea-shell. That whole mighty moor had lain, at some time in its history, between the salt water and the sea strand. 'Is that not enough for you?' said the ruckle. Within a month I had obtained official permission to turn out a few sheep on the moor.

I debated for a long time whether to include that incident. In retrospect it seemed damned daft, according ill with my self-image as a levelheaded farmer and an incisive journalist. But I have never forgotten it and the haunting song comes back to me every year as I help gather the sheep for clipping.

You can hear them long before you see them. An odd, complaining bleat, first from this side, now from that. The agonised wail of a lamb who has lost his mother in the rush. Here and there the shrill whistle, a sharp word of command – and then suddenly over the crest of the hill pours the great living harvest of the moors. Wool, on which the whole of Yorkshire's heritage is built, borne home on the backs of the tough little sheep who now return to the farms in the great annual gatherings to part with their regular contribution to the scheme of things.

As the stream of sheep narrows, as they funnel through the intake gate and spread out again on the other side, lambs and ewes calling to one another after the upheaval, another thought occurs to me. Is this the harvest the old poet had in mind? The riddle tells how the impossible acre must be ploughed with a tup horn and reaped with a sickle of leather. How else might the seeds of this mighty crop be sown, and surely the pair after pair of great boots that gather in the harvest would qualify for the reaping implement.

But somehow on these occasions there is little time for such whimsical debate, and on reflection, perhaps that's no bad thing.

That spring was exceptionally wet. One special day, a Saturday it was, it didn't rain all day. Sun shone on the puddles and steam rose steadily from the sodden woodwork of the sheep pens as I grubbed happily in the vegetable garden.

Suddenly my son cried to me to come and look at a strange bird he had found and I looked over the wall. There on the top rail of the pen was a stranger indeed. The sun glinted on opulent plumage of chestnut and blue and all at once there seemed hundreds of birds, dodging and wheeling, all glowing colours and long, forked tails. Swallows, I told him. 'The swallows are here!' I called to the others.

'One swallow doesn't make a summer,' said my younger son, who quotes in the irritating way some other children pick their noses. But this time I was unquenched. 'There are enough here for two summers,' I said.

Then the rain returned and I have since thought that I would have settled gladly for half a swallow and a little bit of spring.

I had thrown myself wholeheartedly into helping where I could with the regular spring tasks. Old Henry had given me the day-to-day charge of his sheep and I took the job very seriously. The tasks of spring have still to be tackled, whatever the weather.

Much of the seed corn was still in bags, and some of that likely to remain there as the land that was so nearly ready for it so many times lay wet and unworkable. Inorganic fertilisers, presented by the scientists in the form of little granules, are usually easily showered on the meadows from the ugly spinners, but they have the annoying tendency to turn to grey soup if wetted, and then to concrete if left, so the spinners came popping out between showers like little ladies with new perms, one eye on the clouds.

Soon it would be time to mark the lambs. That, too, would need a fine day as, quite apart from the fact that it is bad practice to inoculate them when their fleeces are wet, a whole day handling wet, soggy sheep is a depressing business. In an excess of enthusiasm one day I set myself to catch two of Jim's lambs whose mothers were constant trespassers in Henry's flock. This, I reasoned, would save much time and soul-searching when the main flock were marked.

One of the sheep, an old black ewe whose capacity for slipping through security nets like a seasoned espionage agent kept her from being drafted down-country last autumn, was easily located and her lamb caught without much trouble as he was too young to run fast over the deep heather.

The other, however, a daughter of the first sheep, had lambed a week before, and her little gimmer had all the makings of a true fell-runner.

Several false starts wasted a lot of time. A few tricks like running a group along the side of a wall and using the crook to nab the fugitive, failed miserably because my lamb-catching technique had rusted sadly in 12 months.

I made so many mistakes that it soon became apparent that the only way would be to stick close to the lamb and wait for her to make one.

Round and round we galloped over the heather. Of course, only an idiot would try to catch a lamb on the open moor, but I needed space to be sure I had the right victim and we galloped on.

Up along the rigg we sped, and I quoted bits of 'The Hound of Heaven' under my breath. Astonished neighbours watched from the farm below, in the belief, so one of them told me later, that I was practising for an assault course. The drizzle felt like ice on my red-hot face.

For the umpteenth time she swerved away from me and off in the direction of the peat bog. There were nine other lambs with her and I daren't take my eyes off the few dark speckles above her tail, for fear I couldn't identify her and had to mother her up again. My lungs were bursting and already I was becoming unsure of myself. What if this really wasn't the lamb belonging to the tight-horned shearling who watched uneasily on the skyline. What if . . . but at that moment ten lambs tumbled into a gutter and seconds later nine lambs scrambled out and over the lip of it to disappear in woolly disarray. I had her.

I flung myself full length beside her, with my hand on her back to pin her to the ground, but I needn't have bothered. She had no breath left to run with and neither had I so we sat a bit in the damp gutter. 'You,' I told her 'are your grandmother's girl.' One to carry on the tradition of escapology and steadfast refusal to graze her own pastures, I thought, when the old girl finally goes. I put the correct mark on her fleece.

Or was it. I waited in agony while she made her bouncing way back to the rest of the flock; watched anxiously while the shearling sniffed suspiciously. Then came the hoped-for plunge for the udder, the sheep's mutter of acceptance, and the ecstatic wriggling of the tail that the suckling lamb presents to the watcher as an earnest of satisfaction with the status quo.

Two down, hundreds to go. I was cold and wet again and utterly exhausted. Far down in the valley the cuckoo began to shout. 'Shut up,' I said.

But deep down there was a warmth that the coldest drizzle could not spoil. Time spent among sheep was always a pleasure to me and I was learning daily more and more that would help me when I established, in the autumn, my own moor flock. Then I would surely belong at last to this wild countryside that I was coming to love as though I were native to it.

That summer was a happy one. It was the summer during which Snuff reared her adopted twins and Ernest pig was a source of delight. I bought three chubby Suffolk cross lambs whom we named Doggie, Bertha and Martha, in the hope that their sale in the autumn would put a few pounds into the kitty so that I could buy the Swaledale gimmers I needed to found my flock. But already that flock was beginning to take shape.

It was while I was cutting peat in the first of the long, hot days that I found Georgina. I recognised her as one of the small, late lambs I had marked for Henry. She was lying among the sparse heather on the fringes of the peatbog like a knitted rat that had been left out in the rain and when I lifted her she felt light and dry like crumpled paper. I took her back to Henry, who said I could have her, and I was back where I had started two years before. A drink or two of sweet goat milk brought back her will to live, and she grew.

Then the refuse collector called outside working hours with a delightful little lamb that his girlfriend had bought at Hawes mart with every intention of fattening her for the freezer, but she had fallen in love with the small, solemn creature and asked if I would accept her as a gift – a founder member for my new flock. They called her Lamb Chop and so, in the interests of maintaining some sort of continuity in her life, did I. She answered to it instantly on the first day she came, and she responds to it still. When she grew up it became obvious that she was not a pure Swaledale – there was more than a little of something small and hairy in her ancestry – either a Rough Fell sheep or a Dandie Dinmont – and her horns when they grew resembled nothing so much as the handlebars of a district nurse's bicycle, but for all that first year she was the loveliest sheep we had – which wasn't difficult.

Autumn came, and if I wanted to buy the rest of the flock

at the hill sheep sales, we would have to say goodbye to the three fat Suffolk lambs and the two moor wethers who now stood shoulder-to-shoulder with Snuff, their black foster mother.

Good old Snuff, thrown in as a makeweight with a purchase of pet lambs, nursed through a variety of ailments to grow, albeit slowly, into arguably the ugliest sheep in the north of England. Knock-kneed in front and bow-legged behind, her head carried always at a drunken angle to increase the field of vision of her one functioning, eye, she milked like a bulk tanker all summer and would now have a well-earned rest before having another try to rear a lamb of her own.

However, things had changed since last year, when one only had to screw one's courage to the sticking-place, load the livestock into some suitable transport and away to market. Now the sheep scab regulations were in force and the dipping of all sheep destined for the livestock marts had to take place within 56 days of their movement. So I dipped them.

Using Jim's dipping-tub, I prepared the bathwater carefully, according to the instructions on the tin. I collected up Snuff and the twins and the little Swaledales who were staying with us until they went out to the moor in spring, but of the three Suffolks there was no trace.

They were off in mischief and I knew that to go in search of them would be to have the few I had gathered hopping out of the pen in all directions. They had clearly already twigged that something unusual was afoot and Snuff, who was about to face the water music for the fourth time, was already peering myopically round for an escape route.

I decided to dip what I had to hand and then leave them to drip dry in the draining pen while I fetched back the absentees. Putting off the moment of truth, I stirred the pinkish brew with the end of the dipping-crook, then turned round quickly and seized the nearest victim by the wool under its throat, grabbed another handful above the tail, spun it round and dropped it, behind foremost, into the narrow tub. Only then did I look into the reproachful face below me to see who I had grabbed.

It was Too-Ticky, a tiny lamb I found on the moor with the back of one hind leg mysteriously torn open and bringing with him enough sheep ticks to fill the orchestra stalls at Drury Lane, had they been able to afford a seat each. He hopped round with a splint made from my son's Meccano until he began to show signs of tick pyaemia which necessitated a marathon walk into the village for a precious bottle of penicillin and the leg injury took second place to a week of rather messy minor surgery which he did well to survive. He had only recently joined our little gang and now looked as though he regretted it.

I avoided his eyes as I settled the curve of the crook on the back of his neck and pushed him out of sight. He surfaced, sneezing and I pushed him down again until the wool floated 'free' and I counted grimly. Then I hooked him under the chin with the long tine of the crook and turned him over on to his back. When he struggled right-side-up he was now facing the steps and he made a floundering exit from the maelstrom to stand streaming in the draining-pen, a picture of reproach. Lamb Chop submitted glumly.

Little Georgina, sprightliest of the lot, carried home like a piece of thistledown who was now developing a wicked streak that would gladden the heart of anyone who saw her in her early days here, all pot belly and matchstick legs, was clearly contemplating a scramble up the wall of the catching-fold. She went in next, her cross little face fizzing with outrage before it disappeared into the murky depths of the tub.

Then the first of Snuff's lambs, who was docile enough in the water, but leapt for freedom at the wall beside the draining pen, some of which rumbled into his lap and he had to be rescued before his brother could go in. Then it was Snuff's turn.

I manoeuvred her into the water and then realised that I had made a mistake. The others had taken a fair quantity of the dip out with them and while I could have dipped Lamb Chop easily, three times over, I had to wait for a while until the level crept slowly back up to the mark before I could proceed.

She stood on the bottom of the tub, looking up with an air of amused inquiry and a couple of minutes later she stood with the others in the drainer, but my wellingtons were very full as I set off across the fields to find the Suffolks and the contents played a merry little tune to my toes as it squelched between. I wondered if it would cure athlete's foot.

I sold all that could be spared, and the price seemed good, but when it came to the time of the hill sheep sales, it proved to be woefully inadequate for my purposes. The value of moor gimmer lambs seemed to treble overnight. I could not have afforded more than two at those prices and I confided my disappointment in J.W., who had given me the two foster-lambs for Snuff in the spring. He said he would sort me out four little rejects from his own flock and Bob-the-taxi fetched them out in his ancient trailer. What a sorry collection of woollen mice they were, but they were the best I could afford, and I welcomed them to our house to share with us what looked like being something of a makeshift Christmas.

Why is it always shopping days? Why not garden-digging days, or beer-mat collecting days? Why not even pie-making or pudding-boiling days, ticking slowly away with or without the radio's relentless reminders of how few of them are left between now and Christmas? As if I didn't know!

I wonder if we will ever rediscover a time when Christmas is not something you have to save up for and buy, a time when the days really are measured on something other than cash registers, with their prices mounting higher and higher like precious seconds blinking away on those eerie digital clocks. I'm willing to bet there's nobody reading this who hasn't heard somebody they know saying: 'I dread Christmas', and this sad attitude is clearly encouraged by the lugubrious day-by-day countdown.

The least painful way to observe the approach of Christmas is to use one of those special Advent calendars, with a little door to open for every day of December until the Saviour's arrival on the twenty-fifth, but even these have become expensive, and, at the same time, cheap, with a sort of tinsel pie-crust of Jolly Santa and a lot of cardboard Ho-Ho.

But that year I had a special one. Nancy made it, because she knows I like them, and it was two pages from my rough notebook with the lines running vertically, the doors cut artfully askew with my best scissors and the little pictures lovingly drawn in blunt pencil.

But her face was sad when she gave it to me. She had made her own flour and water paste to stick the two parts together and she had been a little too generous with it. The top layer had oozed slightly out of true. All the pictures were there all right, behind their little doors, but only the top halves were visible. She showed me the baby Jesus, his round bald head smiling happily above a striped football jersey, and an odd number of toes peeping out of the end of the manger, and explained that there was a lamb, too, and cows, but you could no longer see them.

I hugged her and told her that it was a very special calendar. The door into our rather tatty kitchen is made in two halves like a stable door, and I opened the top half. Look out, I told her, and see how lovely the trees look in the snow. Together we looked, and the familiar silhouettes were made magic by a sharp frost. The wall was iced and unspoiled and the whole thing looked like a conventional Christmas card.

Then I opened the bottom-half of the door and we saw the upturned bucket, the trampled yard, all the mess where the hens had eaten their supper, the firewood chippings, the scattered reminders of the sheep and goats and the grubby leavings of a hard day's play. Sometimes, I explained, it's better to see only the top half of the picture and just imagine the rest. She smiled.

The approach to Christmas that year was marked out in a series of little pictures as I whizzed through door after door in the dizzying run-up that even I cannot entirely avoid. A few days' minor illness at the beginning followed by the pleasure of feeling better again. A tussle with a biggish bird of prey over a young starling who was warmed, dried, doctored and released, whole again, in grinning triumph. A dreadful day's shopping, with everything bought except the soap-box cart that Nancy longed for.

Trailing round toyshops to be shown great gleaming things with pedals and hooters that were just not right, and then finding an old pram in the Oxfam shop with a set of fine wheels and meeting a young neighbour – a wizard at making anything from cow-cubicles to bale-carriers – and treasuring his cheerful, 'Why, aye!' as a gift in itself. Wheeling the bargain pram round Northallerton to the ribald comments of smiling friends and manhandling it, after dark, over frozen fields and through poached gateways to the neighbour's workshop.

An evening entertainment at the children's school. Joining in 'While Shepherds Watched' and wondering why God chose shepherds to appear to – after all in the south of England, shepherds used to be buried with a lock of wool pinned to their best smock as an excuse to St Peter for their erratic keeping of the Sabbath.

Coming home in a neighbour's Land-Rover through a very seasonal blizzard. Sitting up late to write a Christmas column. Going outside to see if the sheep were all right; if the new ones had found shelter.

I put on the light at the house corner and the yard was lit up like daylight. Tiny spikelets of snow eddied in a noisy, gusty wind. All the muddle and untidiness was hidden under a kind white cloth.

I called the sheep up and one by one they stepped into the pool of light, blinking frosty lashes. The moor flock I had dreamed of for so long was completed by the arrival of the four 'seconds'. I knew it would have been better to have bought four really good lambs, but the price would have been out of the question, four factory rejects it had to be. They called to one another in the snow.

The lambs collected over the summer months milled boldly around; the four newcomers stayed a little apart. Brownie, with the great patch of red-brown kemp on her hind end. Spotty, with a white patch on top of her head and rather strange horns. Ugly, with her grey face and white legs and Sparrow, smallest of them all, with a white stripe running up her nose that gave her a half-witted expression.

But along with their faults, without which I would never had been able to own them, they brought with them bright eyes, sturdy legs, firm crisp fleeces and the smell of the wind in the heather. An unlikely beginning for the wildest dream a Londoner ever worked for.

The snow settled on my collar, piling against the back of my neck. Slowly, Sparrow detached herself from her companions and came towards me. With all the solemn boldness of the London bird she was named for, she came near enough to push her pinched, whiskery nose into my hand and her rough little lips trembled against my palm in a request for food.

Not so very strange, of course, for small, early-weaned lambs are known for their boldness and cheek as they are forced to explore any avenue that may ensure their survival. But still the tears came, and I swept the silly-looking little creature up in my arms and her gentle tongue licked the salt on my face.

I sat in the snow and held her tight. I thought of the nearness of Christmas. I thought, too, of the help, advice and good humour of the friends and neighbours that had brought me to this point. I thought of the crumpled little advent calendar on the kitchen wall, the mysterious lumpy parcels I'm not supposed to know about – and suddenly it wasn't only just Christmas that was very near.

I set Sparrow down and fondled her fuzzy nose. My fingers were almost frozen stiff and my trousers were soaked. I grinned to myself as a thought suddenly struck me. I knew at last why God chose the shepherds for His messenger to appear to. They were the only folk daft enough to be out at that time of night!

*   *   *

Another spring came. The lambs were now officially old enough to be referred to as hoggs and it was time to train them to live on the moor that was to become their home. One day in particular sticks in my mind. It was too much. There was the kettle, still on the hotplate, but all lopsided, as though it were curtsying to the big enamel saucepan. I snatched it up and it came reluctantly, finally parting company with its entire bottom which bubbled on the radiant plate like volcanic mud, while the top half sizzled in the sink, melting the plug in a final gesture of silent sucks.

Not that it mattered, actually, as it was one of those universal plugs, designed to fit all sinks but mine, over whose outlet it would hover half-heartedly until I put something important to soak, when it would move imperceptibly to one side, letting all the soapy water out and leaving the washing high if not dry in a little pool of jolly mud. Serve it right to perish in a cloud of smoke and an aroma of incinerated wellingtons.

When the sizzling subsided, I picked up the remains of the kettle and peered sorrowfully in through the top and out through the bottom. I could see my feet quite clearly. Then I boiled some water in a saucepan for a cup of tea.

The Founding of the Flock

I had put the makings of a cuppa on the stove before going out to fetch Magnus, the Shetland gelding, back to the house so that he wouldn't turn the daily gathering-in of neighbouring sheep from an orderly procession of ewes and lambs into a great bleating circus by leading the column into the narrow race then turning back through the queue at full gallop. I couldn't find him, and scoured the surrounding fields with no thought of my gallant little kettle. I finally found him where I had looked at first. He was hiding. He is an expert at it.

In daylight, he stands very still in a shadow patch. I believe he holds his breath until I pass him. At night he uses his blackness to wicked advantage, even closing his eyes as the torch catches them. People might assume that he does this as a reaction to the dazzle, but I wonder. When found he comes cheerfully, deeming it beneath his dignity to run away; but he hides.

One of my son's favourite jokes, now worn somewhat thin, is to reply to the question 'Is the kettle boiling?' with an innocent 'No, but the water is.' This was not the case when I returned to the kitchen. The little silvery blobs that bubbled on the hotplate in a soldery sort of way were undeniably kettle and I made a mental note to tell him about it when he came home from school.

I felt small. The night before one of my neighbours had grumbled that my last article contained nothing informative or entertaining; worse, nothing with which he could disagree. That very dinner-time a female friend had told me brightly that she had read one of my articles. She couldn't remember what it had been about; she had bought that paper by mistake, but she had read it. I felt smaller.

Later that morning I trailed slowly up the hill, with two bulging haynets and my pathetically new shepherd's crook, to feed the half-dozen hoggs I had turned out on the moor.

Since they first went, reluctantly, to live on the common, I had taught them to return daily to the gate, where I penned them with a helping of good food until the sheep coming in daily were safely down and the escape routes all shut off for the day. At first, when they had filled themselves, I would walk them further up the moor to show them some more interesting places. I would leave them there, and the following morning a wander up the heather and a good old shout would bring them back to the pen to start all over again.

They suffered from sore eyes when they first went out, and I would search for the currently blind ones, calling and encouraging, bringing them back in ones and twos to the part of the moor they must come to look on as home. It seemed to be working.

But today there was no familiar face peeping through the wire. There was no gallop from the top of the hill in response to my shout. No pirouetting figures falling over each other in their enthusiasm to reach their breakfast. Silence. Here and there a new lamb bleated and an old sheep shifted her position as she waited quietly for the gate to open; but of my own beloved few there was no sign.

I went further up. I searched the three deep gullies where they had chosen to sleep in the early days. I told myself that it was good that they had all gone together, but couldn't dispel the thought that they might have been in mischief; might have been dogged to an unfamiliar part of the moor. I imagined them huddled together in a strange pen, split up and lost, or even rustled. Then I saw them. Sitting in a happy little group by the next gate.

I ran down the track and scolded them roundly. Then I gave my fish-wife shout and they rose, gathered into a crocodile, and began to file after me back to the place I had hoped to find them.

I knew it would soon be time to stop feeding them. That as soon as the moor began to green up after this long, long winter, they must go and take their chance, but on the way back I looked several times over my shoulder to the line of bobbing black faces and when we reached the top of the ploughing above their pen, I broke into a run and they followed me, kicking and galloping, the hand-reared ones bumping and nuzzling, and the cold sweat that had broken out on the palms of my hands warm and sticky now against the varnish of the new crook.

Rough, whiskery faces against my hands. Jostling bodies round the fat haynets. Pride. Joy. Love.

I had been up on the moor less than an hour. Never out of sight of home. Small stuff. But in that time I had known fear, despair, frustration, and bursting happiness.

I imagined myself trying to explain to any more conventional friends what it was that I got out of this apparently ridiculous enterprise. I thought a long time, trying to find a way to express in their terms. How about 'Job satisfaction'?

I knew when I drove my little flock out of the gate for the last time and closed it behind them, leaving them to make their own way on the moor until clipping time, that the coming summer would bring an extra golden pleasure to what had become my favourite task in the farming year. This time some, just a few, of the woolly backs mustered for the shearers would be truly mine. I cherished the thought to myself, afraid to voice it in company for fear of seeming ridiculous, but when the first familiar figures appeared among the smaller, early gathers, the joy was there, just as I had known it would be.

I tried to minimise it, of course, to play it down – but when I took hold of the first of them, while the rest of the team were still preparing the shed for the day's main business and swung her nonchalantly over against my shins muttering something about 'getting her out of the way so as not to hold the job up', I didn't really fool any of those present. They knew that I was really enjoying myself.

The shears sang into the wool on her far shoulder and it fell back white and clean, and I kept my head bent low over my work, but not too low to catch the variety of smiles all round me. The red tag that I had punched into the ear of the little stiff-gaited lamb proclaimed her as number 20 and that was how I entered her in the little blue record book, but she was still Lamb Chop, my present from the dustman and she clung close to me throughout the whole noisy, puzzling day, just as she has done every clipping time since, to the annoyance of everyone else present.

On other days, other names returned – Georgina, Sparrow, Ugly, all of them now good fit shearlings and I clipped them, treated them for worms, marked them firmly and returned them to the heather.

At last came the day of the final gather. I went up with Jim and George and the rest, and we spread out and came down the rigg, with the sheep galloping before us like porridge boiling over the lip of a saucepan and here and there the whiter specks that were the lambs. This time next year some of those specks of thistledown would be mine. The sun was warm and a grouse shrieked with laughter as he whirred out of my way. I remembered something I had been told when I first began collecting my flock together. 'People who keep moor sheep never get to heaven', went the saying, referring to the waywardness of the creatures which caused bad language and bad feeling among the men who kept them, but as I walked along over the soft summer face of Snilesworth moor, I told myself that anyone privileged to have a share in such loveliness had no need of any other heaven than here, than now.

Another Christmas was drawing nearer, and now my shearlings had come home again to the fields round the house for tupping, running with Jim's tups because I couldn't afford one of my own.

When I pointed out to my bank manager that we had been eating rather a lot of porridge lately, he advised me to be careful about getting fat. 'The chance, sir,' I muttered from a distance, 'would be a damn fine thing.'

Do you ever listen to those consumer reports – the ones that tell you from time to time how much The Housewife is paying for a fixed collection of necessities? What they seem to overlook is that when it is the housewife's purse that is fixed, the content of the shopping basket is all that is left to fluctuate, and the dietary intake of the nation's honest poor decreases in direct proportion to the rate of inflation.

It was almost time for the sheep to go back out to the moor when I found one of mine missing at the daily roll-call.

What possessed Sparrow to cross the beck I cannot say for sure, but I have a suspicion that she was kidnapped by an old sheep from the other side which had escaped from a field further up the hill and come down in lone mischief.

Sure enough, the hardest part of the rescue operation was parting her from this elderly mentor, so besotted did they appear to be with one another. I thought grimly to myself as I trailed the pair for the third time round the great intake that if only Sparrow had grown a bit more during the year, the old girl probably wouldn't have taken a fancy to her. I bet she thought she was a lamb.

I went across the beck to fetch her as soon as I had fed all the creatures at home, and it was long gone dinner time when I managed to get the old sheep back with her own flock and was left alone with Sparrow among the brackens. I had believed that when the old one was out of sight, Sparrow would remember who and what I was – maybe even follow me down.

No chance, up and down outside the wall she ran, and up and down inside ran the old one. Calling and bleating, they were for all the world like mother and daughter and weaning time.

It was about three o'clock. I had arranged a complicated trap with gates and time and time again I drove her up to it. I baited it with cake, but the Wensleydale tup on the inside of the gates found it first and was there, his great blue face grinning between the rails, when Sparrow approached it for the last time. With a startled yelp, she fled back down to the beck, in the direction I had been trying to turn her for five hours. I trailed wearily after.

At the bottom, I tried to steer her to the hole in the netting that would trap her so that I could catch her and drag her back across. She trotted past it and went further along the beckside. In an effort to keep above her so she couldn't turn back uphill, I sprinted across some moss-covered rocks, slipped and fell heavily. With a throbbing knee, I limped down to the noisy water and looked bleakly around. She was nowhere in sight.

Once again I set off uphill, sure that she must have gone back. My feet were damp and heavy, and the brackens snatched at them, making every step an effort. There was no sign of Sparrow. I sat in tearful dejection on top of an ancient cinder-hill from whose smooth green top the whole world – or all the bits that mattered then – could be seen. There were a few sheep in the field from which Sparrow had escaped. I hoped they would tempt her back, wherever she was. I could see a handful of sheep in my own yard, and could even tell which was Snuff. A wraith of white mist slid across the picture and then disappeared. Far away on the moor above the house, a great gang of sheep made their way to the sleeping places and I knew it was getting late. I scrambled wearily to my feet and went home.

There was just time to go on up the hill on the other side, to see if there was any Christmas post. Trudging had become automatic and I stumped back home, opening cards as I went. It was surprising how many of them pictured fat, docile sheep.

As I came down the back field, thinking about tea and Christmas cards, I saw a sheep that looked so like Sparrow it was worth investigating. Too tired to chase, I knelt and called her, proffering a fistful of cake, and she came and wolfed it, quite unafraid now that she was back on home ground. Her round eyes pleaded utter innocence but the shiny drippings from her damp fleece told me that she had not long crossed the beck.

Like the shepherd in the parable, I wanted to rejoice with

my neighbours, to celebrate the finding of the one that was lost. All the worry and misery had turned round and was smiling with its other face all over everything. But there wasn't anyone to rejoice with. Except Sparrow. I hugged her smelly wetness and went home.

A performance of *Messiah* and instructions to the children to hush for my favourite aria – He shall feed His flock.

I listened to the sweet setting of the old words and closed my eyes . . . 'and He shall gather the lambs with His arm.' But then came that other phrase . . . 'and gently lead those that are with young.' My grin cracked into a giggle and I whispered to myself: 'The Chance, Lord, would have been a fine thing!'

Little Lambs,
Who Made Thee?

A morning in London. Fog outside. Breath rising visibly in the cold bedroom, making a dew on the folded blanket below my frostbitten nose. My mother calling me. Time to get up; get up and go. Go where? School? or work?

Either way, the lethargy, the lack of incentive to rise at all always comes back very clearly in the small hours, when the alarm clock punches a sharp round hole in the night-time cocoon and I peep out through it to see whatever is peering back at me, waiting for me to get up.

That's exactly how it was on those chill April mornings after my sheep's first winter on the moor. And then, slowly, I remembered, and the days of clinging to the patch of warmth beneath the blanket as if I could lose myself in it until the day ahead tired of looking for me and went away, faded backwards as memory came to life and all at once I would be wide awake, groping for the pile of clothes on the floor. For each day that dawned now could bring with it the first of the moor lambs and there was a special joy in rising early and printing footmarks in the unseasonal hoar-frost on the fields that separated the house from Jim's intake, where I had assembled the tiny flock; a distance quickly covered as soon as there was light enough to see.

I had started contributing a column to our local newspaper at about the time I had started accumulating these few precious sheep, and regular readers often sent good wishes to Lamb Chop, Georgina or Sparrow, and it was somehow an extra burden of responsibility remembering this as I rushed up to check on them first thing in the mornings – as though a sea of unseen faces waited to admonish me if I got it wrong.

One morning I woke to an unusual, uncanny brightness. Horrified that I might have overslept, I was sitting up before my brain had rattled into gear, and it was a moment or two before it registered that the soft light of early morning was reflected double from a generous covering of soft, wet snow, quantities of which were still falling relentlessly.

With a picture of wet and mewling mites shivering in damp drifts, I was out of bed in a flash. Woollen knee-socks pulled up over a pair of ancient corduroys and wellies and balaclava added at the door, I gathered up an armful of the best hay I could find and set off to the intake.

The snow lay lightly on the benty grass like a synthetic topping on a trifle, apologising for cream. I had gone no more than a dozen paces into the field before they were there, all of them, lambless. Waddling forward with a cheerful chorus of greeting were all the names and faces that had become part of my daily routine. One or two cheeky ones pulled at the hay under my arm. I spread it out for them in a sheltered place under the wall.

Sheep. A strange thing for one brought up a townsperson to have become almost obsessed with. I find it so difficult to explain to people what it is about them that draws me and why it was, when I took on the role of a single parent, I took what was left of our lives and began to rebuild them around these simple, quiet creatures. The strange part is that I have never had the slightest difficulty in explaining it to the sheep. Perhaps that's the answer; they can absorb and turn to profit the singlemindedness and old-fashioned loyalty that human beings seem to find hard to accept. There is a satisfaction in shepherding that stems entirely from the characters of the creatures themselves. There is peace in their company and the bond between us is an easy one. If there is such ease in human company I have yet to find it.

When I mustered these few sheep for their pre-lambing injection, Jim watched in great amusement, and asked me how I would manage four hundred sheep if I had them. I don't suppose I would – they would manage me. Oddly, I didn't find the thought tempting.

A couple of weeks previously, one of the familiar faces did not appear when I called them up for their food, and a painstaking search of the moor bottom failed to locate her. My misery pervaded everything else I did. Her image – Georgina it was – seemed always in front of me, the querulous expression on her side-tilted face etched on the inside of my eyeballs. On St Patrick's day I was up early calling and searching, and I heard her call back from the peatbog, no great distance away.

I can remember stumbling across the heather, calling angrily in terms that bespoke anything but affection. I can remember crying a bit on the way back down.

I know that isn't the way the big man does things. He doesn't know 'to an odd 'un' how many sheep he has. A sheep must either be very mischievous or very sick to make herself known to him. Poor chap. He may rear enough mutton to be able to afford to eat it more often than we, but he can't afford the rare luxury of a little stupidity now and then.

The day-to-day management of his livestock is governed by a less immediate set of realities, but as I tended those few sheep in those cold spring mornings, I pitied him, for I suspected the basic motivation was once the same. It is smothered in paper and bound up in barbed wire but it's still there at the bottom of everything. It has to be.

In accordance with the more recent trends in the development of our language I tried to find a single word that would express the whole concept. The best I could come up with was love.

Days passed and still no lambs. I stopped greeting my neighbours with a bright 'No lambs yet!' and waited, only telling them if they asked. I tried to convince myself there was truth in what they always said by way of consolation – that the little lambs were better off where they were with the snow howling down from the moortop on the knife-edged wind and the bitter frosts of those April mornings. But I was beginning to feel the need for some sort of confirmation that the care I had taken all those last months had not been excessive or misplaced. I began to doubt that they were in lamb at all. They were fine and fit – but were they too fine, too fit?

Those were the worries at the back of my mind as I clambered over the gate at the top of the field where they were confined – an unfortunate choice of phrase! – and out onto the moor bottom, for what the more established shepherds called 'a look up the common'. I walked a little way and came upon a gang of George's hoggs, all newly horn-burned and fattened out for their first spring on the moor, just as mine had been twelve months previously. I headed them back so that they wouldn't be in the way when Jim came up to let his ewes down into the fields around my house for the day. I sent them scampering along the track and followed them at a distance, preoccupied with my gloomy forebodings. Then we came upon an old sheep of Jim's with a pair of very new twins. The hoggs gathered round and peered at the babies cuddled in the dead heather until the old ewe's muttered threats sent them scampering on their way again, leaving her in peace with her treasures.

Soon we came upon the main body of George's hoggs, and the stragglers ran in among their friends. Then the whole throng pottered aimlessly up the moor, as silly and irresponsible as any group of youngsters at large, galloping and bumping each other for no reason other than that they felt like it. It had begun to drizzle.

A little way off in the heather, stood a single sheep of Jim's, very still. Something about the way she hung her head made me move towards her. She turned and watched me. I thought better of going too near – if she was about to lamb and had chosen her bed, it would upset her to drive her from it. I could see from a distance that she was a shearling – a sheep in her second year, about to lamb for the first time; the same age as all of my own. I wished her well and walked on across the moor to the old deserted schoolhouse that stands like a little brick shed in the centre of what must have been, in its day, the largest playground in all England. On the way back I made a special detour to see if the little sheep had lambed safely. She hadn't. I had a strong conviction that something was wrong.

She was lying in a shallow gully in the heather, her head sticking over the top. She was looking at me. But the expression in her eyes was not the irritation of a sheep that has been disturbed or the preoccupation of an experienced mother-to-be. It was not even the slight fear of the inexperienced. No, it was a sort of dull hopelessness.

Now that looks even more ridiculous written down than it did when it first crossed my mind. I went a little nearer but could see no sign of a lamb's approach. My conviction grew.

It was now raining steadily, with a mean, thin wind making it seem twice as wet. I stood staring at the sheep. Did I have enough experience to decide what, if anything, was wrong. Would my interference be no more than a nuisance to her, or would my action be like that of the well-meaning motorists who pick up 'lost' lambs and transport them miles to farmsteads while their wandering mothers wail with grief and paddle hopelessly round the places where they left them. I resolved to tell someone else instead.

But everyone was busy. By night, the shearling could

have taken herself off the sleeping-places and might never be found. And if I did not ensure that there was something wrong, how could I justify sending busy people on what might be a wild goose chase. I was almost home when I changed my mind, turned and went back up the moor.

I was so wet now that it didn't matter. When I got to the place where I had left the sheep, she wasn't there. I spied her, wandering aimlessly, on the top of the next ride, only moments before she disappeared from sight. I followed her. Every now and then she would stop and gaze into the distance like a solitary child, daydreaming, meandering vaguely across the great expanse of heather. I thought to myself how lucky she was to have a whole moor to dream in. I remember trying to daydream in our London garden, and how every fantasy was punctuated by the appearance of faces. Parents at windows; neighbours behind the wall, pretending not to see, not to hear. Lizzie Dripping, my parents called me, but it was a hard name to live up to in that goldfish bowl of a garden.

The sheep stopped; her front legs buckled and she went down. Perhaps her lamb was here at last. I stopped and waited, but in a moment she was up again and off. I had to be sure. I circled round and stood in front of her. 'Hello Lizzie Dripping. What's up?' was the best conversational gambit I could find. I caught her without difficulty and examined her, first by simply looking – her lambing had begun, for the water bag containing the lamb was ruptured. I laid her on her side and explored gently for the lamb's presenting parts. I hoped for feet, and a head. Two fingers inserted gently found a soft, flaccid something that seemed at first to bear no relation to the stiff, bony little limbs of a lamb. I drew the tip of it into the daylight and then saw clearly what it was. The end of a tiny white tail. There was clearly no way poor Lizzie Dripping could bring her lamb into the world without skilled assistance, and here I was at a loss. Somehow I had to get that help to her. But how could I ensure that she stayed where she was until I came back with her owner – it would be totally impossible to tell anyone where I had left her; I might not even find her again myself.

'It's no good, Lizzie Dripping' I told her. 'The Mountain must set off in search of Mahomet'.

I tried to drive her, but it was impossible. I swung her up into my arms and started to walk down the moor.

It would have made a better story if we had been miles up the moor, but in fact we were within sight of the road nearly all the way. It would have been more dramatic if it had been snowing instead of merely drizzling albeit coldly. I got her to Jim's farm and left her in good hands. Later that night she was taken to the vet's surgery and safely delivered of a fine gimmer lamb.

The episode was not, however, crowned with total success, because poor Lizzie Dripping hadn't a drop of milk and as soon as she was able she galloped off and deserted her.

But everyone who knew the story was philosophical about it – 'You can never depend on shearlings,' or even 'You never get more than fifty per cent, reared off shearlings . . .' Like the music-hall comedian, though, I did not wish to know that! I returned to my flock of shearlings, to wait and to worry.

It is a matter worthy of record that that lamb survived – they called her Daisy – and she has spent every winter since among my sheep. I look upon her as a special friend and I like to pretend she remembers when everyone else has forgotten.

Of course it had to happen. There is no question that it wouldn't. All the same, on the morning that I found the first of the lambs I had been waiting for for so long, I couldn't quite believe that, at long last, the miracle had truly happened.

Mind you, it wasn't a pretty sight, that first lamb. It was lying under the wall at the top of the field in a slimy puddle. Folds of membrane still clung to it and one of its eyes was held closed by the rapidly solidifying layers. It was his good fortune (for a tup it proved to be) that his mouth and nose had not been similarly obstructed, for none of the small group of sheep that stared, wide-eyed, at the newcomer seemed interested in cleaning off the wrapping and feeding him. Alone he rose stickily to his feet and shook his head. His ears still drooped like a forlorn piglet's and they trembled as he let out a loud, insistent cry to a world that seemed quite unmoved by his presence.

One or two of the sheep looked up at the sound, and one of them, her mouth stuffed with the grass she was cropping, muttered something in an offhand way. A closer examination proved that this sheep had lambed and must be the owner of the little piece of lost property under the wall.

It was all too clear to see what might have happened if I had not had them fastened in a field. I went closer to the sheep and tried to edge her nearer to her lamb, but she shouted a cheerful greeting and came trotting up to see what I had brought her to eat. All the others milled round and the lamb tottered unsteadily into the group, butting at each and every one with his firm, blunt nose, looking for the mother that nature gave him to believe should be there somewhere.

I turned up my collar against the raw morning and withdrew to watch, knowing it was too soon for interference. His mother reached out her nose to the lamb and withdrew it as though she had been burnt. Her companions rallied to her side and pushed him firmly away. Time and again he tried now this sheep, now that, and he was roughly pushed again and again, finally being lifted off his feet by one of them and pushed against the wall. He picked himself up, shook himself, and walked to a small hollow. There he lay down and hung his black, top-heavy head with a shuddering sigh and the ears drooped more miserably than ever. My heart went out to him. The sheep with whom the responsibility lay grazed nearby and mumbled again, her mouth still full. The lamb cried out.

Very slowly, very cautiously, she moved towards him. He cried again. I saw her reach forward with her lips and tongue outstretched and make the first, rough contact with the knobby little spine. He stretched ecstatically and shook his head. Once more he cried and the sheep, startled, leapt away from him and returned to her patch of grass as though grazing were about to be made illegal.

The lamb knew now, though, and rose to his feet. With a firmness of step amazing in a creature so new to the world, he walked purposefully towards his mother. But when she saw him coming she ran away.

The early sun strengthened and the mist dispersed. I knew there was no rush. There would be time enough for a do-or-die confrontation when the situation became desperate. At home there were baths to run, breakfasts to make and youngsters of my own to feed and get off to school. I went back home, looking back at the last moment to see how things were. The sheep was alternately retreating and advancing, wanting her lamb, yet terrified of it, and I left the problem to her maternal instincts and his determination to sort out between them.

But after an hour or so, things were no better. The lamb was still uncleaned and the sheep unsuckled. It was time to take a hand.

I gathered all the sheep into the pen in the corner of the field then put all the others outside. I went back for the lamb and put him into the restricted space with his mother – that would even up the odds a little – and left them, after rubbing the worst of the mess off his face.

An hour later the magic had begun to work. He looked immeasurably cleaner and she muttered constantly to him, putting the finishing touches to his clean white coat. But he still hadn't sucked. Every time he approached her udder she butted him away and he was getting weak. I caught the sheep and forced the issue.

Twice more that day I connected the lamb to his food

supply. As night drew near she still hadn't accepted him spontaneously and I went for the pup, aiming to try the age-old method of forcing her into defending her lamb from a dog. As we approached the pen, a group of tourists, who had left their car parked alongside the pen, were perched on the rails taking a photograph of them. I fumed inwardly and moved faster towards the pen.

One of the adults stepped down into the pen and knelt to take another picture. Whatever next? I imagined him telling one of the children to pick up the lamb – 'let's get one of Jimmy holding it to send to Aunty Flo . . .' As I ran nearer they drifted back to their car and drove off.

I walked the last few yards and looked over the rails. There was good old Ugly, staring after the departing intruders with her lamb tucked safely beneath her, sucking away for all he was worth. His tail wriggled with delight. The battle was over and everybody had won.

That night, Nancy asked me what we were going to call the lamb. I explained that now the flock was established the sheep were no longer pets, and it would be better if we simply stuck to numbers. In the records the newcomer was HH 24/34, and this would be a much more businesslike way of describing him. She said she understood. I put my arm round her – 'Let's call him Primo' I suggested.

Lambing, which had taken so long to get started, suddenly almost over and I seemed to have done very well. Every sheep had a lamb to follow her, with only two near misses.

Poor Spotty, had a small and beautiful gimmer lamb quite early on in the proceedings, although rather late in that particular day. She was a little afraid of her at first and it was beginning to get dark before she allowed the persistent mite to suck unmolested. It was moonlight when I went for my final check. All seemed well.

The following morning, however, the lamb was unable to stand and in obvious pain and poor Spotty was distracted with worry, nosing and gentling the lamb she had only just come to love. My own feelings can be well imagined.

It was early in the morning and the ground was whitened with a late but cruel frost. I carried the lamb as gently as I could and Spotty followed, calling sadly. Back at the house I made them a bed in an outbuilding and debated whether I should call the vet. After all, the newborn lamb is a vulnerable thing at the best of times, and even with the rising prices for store and fat lambs, a visit could probably not be justified financially. But that wasn't the point. This was one of so few lambs. Spotty wanted her. I wanted her. She was part of the future. I went to the telephone.

I called at Jim's house for the purpose, and when he and George heard the story, a day's corn-drilling was postponed for an hour or two while they ferried me, Spotty and the little patient to the surgery at Northallerton.

Injections, medicine, hope, prayer, nursing and then the despair that makes the final success all the sweeter. She lived. I think the vet was surprised.

When Lamb Chop produced a large and beautiful lamb, the last but one to arrive, I did not interfere, although the process took a long time. On this occasion, though I should have done. How easy it is to be wise in retrospect. So tired and weakened was poor Lamb Chop that she had neither the energy nor the inclination to lick the newcomer. I resuscitated it and took the pair of them down to the same building, which was now a full-scale post-natal ward. I watched and waited, but clearly all was not well with this one, either.

*   *   *

This time the vet came out. He gave us much practical help as possible, together with unbegrudged time for investigation and discussion. I felt happier knowing that I had done my best but sure, nonetheless, in a flat sort of way, that it wasn't going to be good enough. She died at about two in the morning. The consolation was that Lamb Chop, unlike Spotty, couldn't give a monkey's.

I rose early, despite the late night. From the hill behind the house I could hear Lamb Chop grumbling at her continued imprisonment. I had to make up my mind.

The question was, should I go out of my way to get another lamb, an orphan or weakling, for her. Economically, the answer was yes. She had been generously treated all winter and was well supplied with milk. It would be bad husbandry to let her waste it all. But somehow I hated the thought of doing such a thing for that reason alone. It seemed greedy. When Snuff lost her first lamb, I got her two little ones and she grew to love them with the fierce, maternal possessiveness that is a lamb's greatest safeguard. Perhaps dear, lackadaisical Lamb Chop would find similar fulfilment. I decided to walk over the moor to the farm of the man who gave Snuff her foster-lambs. If he had a pair of twins to split or an orphan to spare, I could offer it a generous food supply. If not, I would let her go back to the moor without a lamb.

With Andrew's sports bag hanging empty on my shoulder, I set off, and arrived eventually at his door, footsore. No one was about, save a black cat, who seemed hopeful that her master might return at lunchtime from wherever he was. Assorted beasts gave me their undivided attention for a short while before wandering back to their grazing. In the fields at either side of the road, sheep and lambs wandered, alternatively guzzling or merely enjoying the first fine day in what seemed ages. One especially tiny lamb slept right on the road, responding to my gentle poke with a gusty sigh. That's the sort of lamb I had in mind. A real tiddler, with all the world to grow in. He seemed to belong to a hogg, or yearling, who watched with wary detachment from nearby. I touched his tiny round head with one finger, but he did not wake.

I finally caught up with my friend at his sister's house

nearby and he assured me that he had the very lamb. One of a pair of twins born to a favourite hogg. I left with the same lamb I had coveted tucked inside the sports bag. On the way home I touched his fuzzy head from time to time. I hoped Lamb Chop would like him as much as I did.

She didn't. She was as awkward as Snuff had been, clearly offended at the presumption of the young stranger in touching her tender udder. He, on the other hand, was quite different from the two lambs I had offered Snuff; whereas they were keen to avail themselves of the facilities, he clearly wanted nothing to do with the arrangement. I sat Lamb Chop on her hind end, and reached for him to connect him to the teat, but he scooted round the building like a thing possessed while I grabbed occasionally from the middle. I had to let the sheep get up and secure the lamb before starting all over again.

It was easier said than done. I was reminded all at once of a large, bleary-eyed, yellow-toothed rat which I had once met in my grandmother's outside lavatory. I was in what might be described as a position of disadvantage when I saw him, and sat still until cramp forced me to try a break for freedom.

My grandmother never locked the lavatory door. In fact she had an old flat-iron with which to prop it open because she liked the view across the meadow. I, however, felt a town child's insecurity in such a situation and always bolted it firmly. On this occasion I regretted it. As I fumbled with the little bolt, the rat panicked and ran. Round and round the floor it went, sometimes running a little way up the wall like a stunt rider, pattering over my sandalled feet at each circuit until I released myself and ran back to Gran's kitchen as though all hell were behind me.

After watching for a while the wretched lamb's similar performance I called him Bograt, which name he retained until we parted company. Having done battle simultaneously with Lamb Chop's pedalling hind legs and his tiny clenched jaws, I regretted at first, having decided to subject either of them to this indignity. But by the end of the week she seemed to have decided that she really did like the idea of a lamb of her own, and he scuttled in below her wool with the same determination he applied to escaping her only a day or two before. As they say in these parts, 'it was right'.

To Further a Field

Very early on in the story of my venture into hill farming, it became apparent that one of the prerequisites for success was a little land. I had been given the vital permission to keep sheep on the moor, and nobody could object to them, or threaten them, or challenge their rights to be anywhere at all on the stern face of the gaunt moonscape that dominated the dale. It gave me rights too – I could go sheepgathering with my nearest neighbour Jim and his son George as I was now officially 'turning out on t'bottom end'. I could rebuild walls and unstop ditches, because I had a stake in the moor at last.

But I was a long way from being fully independent. Jim allowed my sheep to run with his at tupping time and lent me a field to lamb them in for the first couple of years, but the wind was changing. The first swingeing rent increases left us all reeling. My own rent went up four hundred per cent at one massive blow, even after the intervention of the council arbitrator, who whittled two hundred a year off the managers' original demand.

That spring I put my sheep into Jim's intake to lamb, as I had done the two previous years. 'Intake' is the local expression for reclaimed moorland. Intakes are the rough fields that form a halfway house on hill farms between the more intensively husbanded 'inside land' and the surrounding moors, on which the grazing rights are common to all those holding a 'stray'. In recent years many of the old intakes have become every bit as good and productive as the inside land, since each farmer is forced to make the maximum use of all he has. But Jim's intake at lambing time doesn't offer a lot, since he uses it in winter to fold his hoggs at night, and by the time they are turned out and lambing begins, all the sheltered places are inches deep in deposits of natural fertiliser that would gladden the heart of any tomato grower. That spring was a wet one, and matters were worse than usual, with most of the field trampled to depressing peaty slurry. However, the field is divided by the road that runs through the dale, and the lower half was not so badly poached. Jim said I could use that if I wanted to. I decided to leave the sheep in the top half until they were actually due to lamb and then move them down.

The day before the first one was due, I told Jim I was going to shift the sheep. Without looking me in the eyes, he asked if I thought that that was really a good idea. 'Aren't you afraid they might get staggers?' he said. 'Of course not,' I said, laughing. Old Jim was having me on again. Did he think I'd learned nothing over the years? Staggers is a metabolic disease caused by a shortage of the mineral magnesium. This can be triggered in a variety of ways, but there is a natural decline in the magnesium in spring, and they can die if suddenly introduced to young rapidly growing grass, especially grass that had had a liberal dosing with artificial fertilisers.

But who did Jim think he was kidding? The lower half of that intake was no rapidly growing pasture. It was just cleaner than the upper bit, no more. And men on Yorkshire hill farms don't start throwing expensive artificial fertilisers around so early in the year, especially when it is as cold and wet as it was then. I was puzzled and said so. 'Think about it' mumbled Jim, and I stared after his retreating figure, knowing that there was something that I should grasp, that I should understand, but not quite knowing what it was. I thought about it.

The only thing that was completely obvious to me was that, for some reason, Jim did not want me to put my sheep in that field. Therefore, since it really was Jim's field, I told him I'd decided against it. I didn't want him to think, though, that I believed the bit about staggers, and determined to tell him so when I saw him next. I was still puzzled and unhappy. It was good of Jim to let me have half of the intake but why not all of it, as he had promised. I went for a walk up the moor, feeling hard-done-by.

Looking down into valley I saw that the lower half of the intake was scattered with white dots. I went to investigate. Jim had given the field to his precious blue-faced Leicesters and the hurt took my breath away. So much for staggers. I ran out of the gate and up the moor until my legs were weak and finally lay in the heather, probing at the sore spot like a cavity in a tooth, very carefully, like an exploring tongue, until I could locate the pain and come to terms with it.

At first all I could say to myself was 'why had he done it to me?' and I sobbed like a disappointed child. Then I realised that this was the thing I had dreaded for so long; the shadow that had been creeping towards me ever since I came. The real world had caught up with us all at last and even Jim, whose whole gentle philosophy of live-and-let-live had typified all that was best in the hill farmer's way of life, had been forced into stocking to the very limits of his holding. Jim needed every blade of grass he could grow for his own stock, every suckler cow and every pedigree ewe his land could possibly carry, just to hold on to what he had worked for all his life. The idyll was over and the Arcadia I believed I had found was gone forever. I understood at last, but the pity of it was I could never tell Jim. To do so would have been to call his bluff over the staggers which would have been, in the circumstances, unpardonable.

At that time, Old Henry, whose sheep I had looked after

a year or two before, decided to take things a bit easier and gave up most of his land and all his moor sheep, keeping just two or three fields near his house. Many a landlord would have edged the old couple out and let the house at a huge rent, but not Our Lordship, bless him.

There remained, though, the vexed question of what was to happen to that portion of the land for which old Henry had no further use. I dared to hope. Not that I expected miracles. The fields that were to be re-allocated were far too valuable for me to be considered as their tenant. There was no way I could afford to lime and fertilise even the smallest of them. But there was a rough, unfenced intake which had possibilities, and a tiny, stony paddock that was only just better than nothing. I asked His Lordship tentatively.

But the fate of all Old Henry's holding had already been decided and I tried hard to hide my disappointment.

Now I heard rumblings of disquiet as approaches were made here and there, for even friendship did not stretch far enough to allow even the smallest corner of any man's hard-won holding to be handed over to anyone else, especially someone whose status wavered as mine did, and while I loved His Lordship for trying, I found the backlash of his efforts hard to live with. It was as if I'd been bold enough to tug at Jim's sleeve and ask him for an acre, as if I'd suggested that George had too much and could spare some for me. I felt as if nothing would ever be as it had been before. Trying was one thing; succeeding another.

Several weeks later, the estate manager stopped me on the road, to tell me officially that His Lordship had instructed him to find me some land. After much thought, he said, he could offer me one of two stretches of uncultivated roadside if I cared to consider reclaiming it. Then he drove away.

One of the strange phenomena of the countryside is the swirl of silence that closes around a pedestrian on an open road immediately after the departure of a vehicle. It's like the visible self-adjustment of a bowl of custard when one scoops out a single spoonful. It was just such a sticky quiet that held me fast for a few moments as the blue car disappeared round the corner. Numb. This was it; this was what I had wanted. I was going to have my land, and not only with His Lordship's blessing, but without taking it away from any of the other farmers.

Then, very slowly, there came a picture of the two pieces of land in question. A patch of head-high bracken at the lower side of the road, a patch of arid scrub on the high side, punctuated here and there with stunted birches and separated from the moor by a wire fence. Neither of them could have been further from the little field I had in mind, and I walked slowly back along the road to get another look at them, in the hope that they were not as bad as I remembered. They were worse.

The lower area had grown nothing but bracken for years. Below it a mixed plantation of immature trees stretched down to meet Jim's land, and above it, across the road, was a sandstone quarry which visitors used as a car park and picnic place in summer. As I picked sadly among the debris I realised where the visitors deposited their bottles, tin cans and plastic bags, out of sight and out of mind. Further from the road, nearer the edge of the wood, more secretive souls had withdrawn to enjoy the fruits of love. The skins were everywhere. Among the nettles in an overgrown ditch I found a huge pair of pink knickers. Even so, it was a marginally better proposition than the higher piece of ground. At least it was flat. The other sloped up to the moor at a crazy angle, and stopped high above the road in a sort of sandstone cliff, bristling with bilberry wires and neglected heather. A gathering of windswept birches had spindled up since the moor fence had been built, sparing them from the ubiquitous sheep-teeth which spoilt the chances of any young trees above it. From top to bottom ran a great natural gully that took floodwater from the moor on its way down to the river. But at either side small planted areas, intended to protect the road from drifting snow, were beginning to fill up. I imagined that I was a sheep. And that it was winter. On that piece of ground I would be safe from the cruel northerly winds, tucked in among the little birches. As the plantations grew up, I would be sheltered from the west and from the east. But however could I reclaim such a craggy little corner? I went back again to the lower piece of ground. The wood along the bottom gave shelter from the southerly gales. I would ask for both pieces. After all, nobody else wanted them, and the battle to turn them into pastureland would be between me and nature, and the stirrings of bad feeling between me and my neighbours would be stilled. The hollow ache of disappointment pushed firmly to the back of my mind, I went to tell Jim and Flora. But it came out all wrong. It sounded as though I were boasting about my good luck but what I was really trying to do was to tell them that I knew what had been going on, that I cared. That I didn't want to take anything on a plate, that I was prepared to work for what I needed. After all, ever since I arrived in the dale I had fought harder for the right to offer my assistance to my neighbours than for almost anything else. I told them and waited. I saw something that looked suspiciously like jealousy in Flora's eyes, but Jim smiled and said 'You jammy bugger', and I dared to hope that he understood.

All the same, when I left and went slowly home, the artificial elation was all gone. How silly I must have looked, reaching out like an eager puppy to grasp the mucky end of the stick. But having taken hold, I must hang on. I went back up to the road and started planning the conversion of the first, the lower, field. Striding out rough yards, I measured the line of the fence.

The following summer there was a lot of discussion in the country papers about the spraying of bracken. It's a subject that recurs automatically at this time of year.

Opinions varied, some saying that bracken should be exterminated, it being neither use nor ornament, others claiming that it should be left alone as a natural part of the environment – a difficult question.

I suppose if you hold rigidly to the precept that everything has its place and purpose in the scheme of things, the wholesale destruction of acres of natural greenery is too terrible to contemplate, but although I have very strong sympathies with conservationists in most of their spheres of activity, I cannot find it in my heart to extend any sympathy at all to the ubiquitous bracken.

It reminds me of flies. It has been said 'God in His wisdom made the fly and then forgot to tell us why.' I remember reading somewhere of a tribe of Bedouin who veil their faces lest they swallow a fly and thereby destroy a life and endanger their immortal souls.

I approved inwardly – 'fall of the sparrow' and all that – because at that time I couldn't see any real harm that a fly could do to justify man's hatred of him.

I mean, little fruit flies have taught the facts of life to generations of youngsters who have then been turned loose to create their own fictions to go with them. That was before I saw my first sheep struck by blow flies.

A little scratch had attracted them to the ewe's back and there, on the sore place, they had laid their eggs. What I saw as the wool was clipped away was horrifying in the extreme.

A great gathering of fat maggots feasted on the living flesh of the poor sheep; you could hear them clicking and rustling in the ravaged tissue, see the vertebrae laid bare beneath.

They were killed by a liberal application of Jeyes fluid and further damage prevented by a generous layer of Stockholm tar, but as the poor sheep tottered away, still crazed with pain, I ground the last of the living maggots with my heel and wondered why.

And now, why bracken? Although most livestock find it distasteful, some will eat it and it seems that those tempted to try it sometimes develop a taste for it that becomes, in time, a craving. They eat more and more, unable to leave it alone, while the poisons it contains do their terrible work on the creature's system.

The horse and the pig suffer nervous disturbance through the vitamin deficiency caused by the destruction of thiamin in their bodies, but the poor ruminants – cattle, sheep and goats – whose internal arrangements are different, are affected by another toxin which destroys their bone marrow and eats away their intestine, so that portions of the gut wall are passed out of their bodies. The pain can be imagined.

Sometimes these two abominations get together, the brackens harbouring the suffering sheep while the flies go about their nasty business. In the damp, dark places beneath them, too, lurks the sheep tick, another parasitic killer.

But in winter, and at lambing time, when there might be some benefit in their shelter, where are the brackens then? Safe under the ground.

I truly believed that the big snows of the preceding winter had actually protected the brackens from the usual damage by freezing, making this year's growth especially luxuriant, the great green fingers cocking a snook at the punished heather and the depleted flocks.

That's what I told myself as I fought my way through great, coarse fronds higher than I am, with the nozzle of the knapsack sprayer peeping above them like the conning tower of a submarine.

The Asulox solution I was using was sticky on my skin, I was soaked because the sprayer leaked, and the webbing straps had scoured the skin off my shoulders, but I searched among the brackens with the little brass nozzle, almost one frond at a time, pretending they were alien invaders withering before my space-gun.

Not that they withered visibly as they would have done with most weedkillers. Asulox works by travelling down through their systems, poisoning their vital parts below the ground, killing them slowly like Jim's little Galloway calf who died in my arms in the blessed twilight of the morphine from the vet's bag.

Some people would mourn the brackens – the debris I found as I quartered the area bore witness to the fact that summer visitors had used them for a variety of purposes. Now they would have to go elsewhere. I had fenced, and sprayed this little area to make safe grazing for the Drysdale sheep.

Next spring I would sow grass seeds in the worst places and feed the sward in the better ones. Already there were grasses growing – cocksfoot and Yorkshire fog, with little patches of clover and the ribwort that sheep love.

Every so often I went and stood in my field, just looking. Not that there was much to see. A great deal of bracken, now fading fast and crushed to slimy debris in the wheelings of the lime spreader that emptied a part load by special request, huge thistles and great tufts of bilberries and more heather than I would like – but if I closed my eyes I could see the whole thing covered with cocksfoot, timothy and clover.

I should have to make my field come true from the only available acre, but, like the little engine, I could – and I would.

The following spring, Jim bought himself a rotovator.

Access to the field was to be by way of a gate. I was given a huge oak gate by friends in the village, but it was an enormous antique, on which generations of children had hung, peeping at the traffic, and swung back and forth in rosy rows, and while I loved it and was happy to save it from ignominious burial under a pile of rubble, I had to own that it was much more in keeping with the approach to Jim's farm than to our field, especially as the post with which I had been supplied was a larch of less than generous proportions, and the idea of its supporting such a monument was out of the question. Jim's house, on the other hand, was guarded from the world by a lightweight metal gate which was in need of a lick of paint. So we swapped.

Now at the time I was anxious to finish the job of sinking the larch post, finishing the fence off neatly, and hanging the gate. Jim, on the other hand, was busy doing something seasonal and couldn't see any need for speed. I suppose I must have pushed a little hard, because Jim seemed unnecessarily gruff when I told him I needed the new gate so I could measure up for the post. He put on his stressed expression and said he failed to see the need for haste. The metal gate was the same size as the wooden one. I dared not argue.

I had made one hell of a hole to take that gatepost. I had filled it in and tamped the soil down around the lonely larch – but when I heaved the great oak gate up alongside it, there wasn't enough post sticking up; the gate stood higher than the post. If the metal gate were really and truly the same size, then the post had to come out.

I dug out the post, partly filled the hole, reset the post, and, in the fullness of time, Jim brought on the metal gate and we effected the exchange. When I set the metal gate up beside the post, there wasn't enough gate sticking up; the post stood higher than the gate – by about eighteen unsightly inches. I hung that gate perfectly. It swung like a dream, it clicked perfectly shut, snug against the end-post of the fence. But the great lump of gatepost haunted me and I fumed. Jim viewed the job.

'If they won't jump the gate, they won't jump the post,' he said, grinning and I poured forth all the bottled-up frustration that had grown each time I set my eyes on that positive flagpole of excess timber, grinning at me over the wall of the adjoining field. Jim was hinting that I hadn't got that post deep enough, when I knew damned well that I had sunk it every bit as well as he could have done. For once I had done something right and now nobody would know. 'You miserable old bugger,' I addressed him, lapsing into the vernacular, 'you told me those gates were the same size!' 'So they are,' said he, 'they're both twelve foot,' and he maintained that the size of a gate is only a matter of width. Height, he claimed, is of no consequence. I did not, do not and never will believe him, but the gatepost stands to this day as a monument to that misunderstanding and a constant reminder to me never, ever, to take anything for granted especially when told by a fellow-farmer.

I was unreasonably disappointed in Jim. After all, he had laughed as loud as anyone when I told the story of what happened when I went to buy the net for the fence. I had measured in yards the length of my projected boundary, and went into the agricultural merchant's treasurehouse of wares, enjoying the fact that, for once, I was going to be buying something of more consequence than a handful of nails or a pair of wellies. 'How much', I asked, 'per yard is your heavy-duty pignet?' The miserable fellow stared at me for a moment or two, obviously savouring his position of superiority, before replying that this was a question he could not answer. Another Churchillian pause preceded the coup de grâce. 'We're metric now. How many *metres* would you want?'

I had to confess that, without much calculation better done in private, I couldn't really say. But at least I could do my calculations from a position of strength if I knew the price of the commodity. 'How much', I asked, 'is it per metre?' 'That depends,' he said loftily, 'on whether you want the three foot or the three foot six.' I withdrew, grinning.

Whether it was conscience or not, I couldn't say, but Jim lent me both his new rotovator and his younger son, Sid, and together they roared back and forth across the wasteland, chewing the bracken litter and the lumps of lime – and, quite coincidentally, the main telephone cable – into a tilth fit for grass seeds.

Like the first fragile fuzz on a young lad's upper lip, those precious seeds changed the face of that little field. Gradually, as the warm, wet days continued, they green-glossed the surface that had sported, until now no more than dense bracken and bilberry wires. And with them, a dream was coming true.

Not that it was easy. No good fairy came and did it overnight and the only wand waved over the area was the bow of Jim's old fiddle drill, but it seemed to have done the trick.

Have you ever seen a fiddle drill? It's the sort of thing that turns up in quizzes about farming bygones; if the instructions on the side have worn off, I think most people would be hard put to it to guess its purpose. It consists of a cloth bag, the bottom of which is supported on a wooden frame with a floor that slopes to allow the contents to dribble out on to a metal thing that looks like a kiddies' windmill. This last is whizzed round by the energetic to-and-froing of a wooden bow which spins a wooden bobbin by means of a leather thong. Not exactly the sort of thing you associate with Yehudi Menuhin, but at a distance it looks somewhat similar.

The idea is that you fill the bag with seeds for broadcast sowing and then, controlling the rate of dribble with a metal lever at the side of the apparatus, you stride out over the area to be sown, fiddling like a thing possessed. It took me a long time to work out what difference it would make to the operation that I had legs only half the length of the machine's owner, and arms in proportion. Did it matter what speed I went at?

I decided that the only thing that mattered was to move in a predetermined rhythm – an arm-and-a-leg, an arm-and-a-leg and to keep it up no matter what happened, even at the risk of being reported to the Royal Commission on Silly Walks. It all works perfectly well, you see, if you steadfastly ignore the funny side of the operation. If your sense of the ridiculous is awoken at any stage, you're done for.

If you stop for any reason at all, the little seeds continue to pour out onto the spinner. There is a thing to shut them off with, but that's the last thing that occurs to you when something happens to interrupt operations.

The first thing that stopped me was young Sid who had rotovated the field for me. I could see him waving his arms and trying to tell me something. I had both hands occupied with the fiddle drill, which was slung round my shoulder on a webbing strap so that I couldn't wave. I stopped and smiled instead. He gesticulated wildly and I stood gaping, trying to guess what it was he wanted. Finally he came floundering over the newly-cultivated soil, shouting for all he was worth. 'Don't forget,' he was saying, 'to put it out of gear if you stop.' I looked at the pile of seeds at my feet and nodded, smiling sweetly.

I had to stop an amazing number of times. My arms were apparently not long enough to haul out the bow to its fullest extent, and in attempting to do so I repeatedly entangled the thong in the flights of the spinner. The fact that the drill itself was something of an antique prevented me from giving it a good old yank and it always resulted in a few moments' panic with seeds hissing out all over the place, before I remembered to shut off the outlet.

Once or twice I fell flat on my face. Soil that has been rotovated rather than ploughed is very light and spongy and walking over it to sow the seeds was hazardous in the extreme. After I had sown it, it was rolled several times, and soon felt quite normal underfoot, but while I was trying to propel myself and the dreaded instrument up and down it, it had the consistency of sponge pudding and I could imagine what it must be like to be an ant, fallen into someone's pocket and scurrying along through a great depth of fluff.

Boobs, even small ones, are a hazard, too. Whoever designed the fiddle drill never intended it to be operated by a female. Bows in general are difficult for women and I remembered the legendary Amazons, who solved the problem by resorting to unilateral amputation. In my case the problem was solved by breathing in and leaning forward, which added to the farcical aspect of the procedure.

But I managed, and the little seeds thrived and grew.

Along the top of the field, though, things were not so good. I had run out of seeds and borrowed some from George. The seeds were old and they failed. I bought some more.

I had to decide whether to borrow the fiddle drill again, and decided that I would manage without, I resorted to an even older method, filling a small bucket with the seeds and broadcasting them by hand. This time I had a friend to help me.

The warm, west wind blew strong and steady at my back as I stepped out to begin sowing. I filled my fist with as many seeds as I could hold and swung my arm in an easy arc, letting the seeds trickle through my fingers, cool and silky as fine oatmeal. Buoyed up on the wind they eddied and spun, falling gently to the warm, wet earth in an even drift. 'Did you sow them by hand?' asked Jim. 'Yes,' said I. But the mere monosyllable couldn't describe the wonderful feeling of omnipotence, of having, of owning, of loving the little acre I'd worked so hard for. Even as I recalled the experience I could feel again the strong pull of the wind, taking and carrying my precious seeds and the heady feeling as they whirled away. 'Yes,' I said again. 'And by golly, they did go!'

A year later I went fencing. Not with foil or epee but with crowbar, monkey strainers and what is known in the trade as a universal tool.

I now confide freely that I have done a good bit of private weeping over parts of the job that seemed just too huge for a middle-aged mother to cope with. But it's done. 150 metres of fairly satisfactory and apparently stockproof fencing, and I did it all by myself.

Jim and George had put up my first fence; I assisted, gathering ideas if not experience, and Flora and Sandra hovered on the periphery, but this time I was on my own.

By now we referred to that first enclosure as 'the field' as though it had always been part of our lives. Our gimmer hoggs spent a month or so in it while the tups were at large nearby and learned there the basic necessities for members of the Drysdale flock. They grew fit and bouncy.

Winter, though, taught me a hard, sad lesson. While I suffered no losses among the sheep actually on the moor, when I turned out my fine, fat hoggs round about lambing time, they faded to gaunt shadows and the smallest died, unable to make a living on the black, inhospitable moor.

Now I was determined that the hoggs should begin to acclimatise to their future home as soon after Christmas as possible. Sound husbandry but, as things stood, a practical impossibility.

The hoggs stayed in the field on the low side of the road while on the high side the moor stretched, waiting for them. It might as well have been a million miles away for all the good it was.

You see, to get on to the moor they had to go out through a gate, and this they could not do at this time of year, in fairness to my neighbours. There are four gates near my home, all known locally by the names of the farmers who have the right to 'turn out' there. To use any one of them would mean disrupting the sheep at present using them and upsetting carefully established routines that had been built up over many years.

I had to choose whether to wait again, and turn the hoggs out while the adult sheep were in for lambing, with the attendant risks I had learned, or to go ahead and fence that other piece of land to make a rough intake with access to the moor for their exclusive use. I decided to try.

Our landlord, whose encouragement has been our mainstay, gave his blessing to the venture. Rosalie's piglets bought the raw materials. I planned a fence that would look as unobtrusive as possible and then set out to recruit assistance.

I had picked a bad time of year and an unfortunate climate of opinion. I waited a while but could foresee no improvement so I decided to make a start myself. I began to dig the holes for the straining posts and soon hit a big, yellow snag.

The top few inches of the terrain consisted of soft bracken litter, followed by even fewer inches of pinky-grey sand. Below that was solid yellow sandstone into which a spade would not go unless its entry was preceded by much energetic grovelling with the pin from an old boartether which serves me as a crowbar.

I had done this job before, under supervision. I knew that when it came to pounding the spoil back round the post my strength would be found wanting, so a deep, narrow hole was needed. The most difficult part of the enterprise was getting the bits out of the bottom of the hole. I fitted the tools to the job and anyone who saw me trotting down the road with a feedbag and a fireshovel must have been puzzled indeed, never dreaming that I needed the bag to lie prone on while I wangled the bits out with the shovel. But I did it.

Once the posts were as firm as I could get them, I had to add a strut to each one; let into the post at the top and wedged against a stone at the bottom, these would prevent the posts from being pulled sideways when the wire was strained tight. I went to ask George which side they should go. I knew perfectly well, but I hoped he would come and demonstrate because my joinery leaves much to be desired. How could I, who had my work cut out to make a saw horse, fashion a correctly angled strut that would fit into a similarly angled groove?

I went home clutching a rough sketch on the back of an envelope. The following day, with our Nancy applying her not-inconsiderable might to the other end of the bow-saw, I set up my first few struts, and they weren't bad.

I wouldn't go so far as to say that they were good and to date you are the only people apart from myself who know that one of them let me down and had to be re-done. A day later, though, some of the wire was up. It took me an age to fathom out how to hook on the monkey strainers and even longer to persuade them to let go again, but I enjoyed using them, watching the jolly little robot hands hauling in the slack. But I hadn't the nerve to strain it as tight as I should have done, the stakes weren't as straight as I wanted them to be, and my arms ached unbearably from swinging the great sledgehammer that had driven them grudgingly inch by inch into the unrelenting subsoil. I cried myself to sleep.

The following day I got the second roll of wire to the site, took a deep breath and began again. This time I was straining the wire to a good, fat post, buried to half its height and I pulled the top strand singing-taut with a strange new confidence. A passing neighbour had pronounced my first effort not too bad and my heart had grown again from the shrivelled little walnut that stuck in my throat all through the night before.

I finished my fence in a snowstorm. I spanned a tricky ditch in fine style and two more neighbours said they 'couldn't fault it'.

But I could. I wish I could go back and put up the first section with the knowledge and experience I had gained by the end of the job.

The last thing needed was a gate out onto the moor, but there finance failed me. I made do by removing a triangular portion of wire between a strut and a straining post of the original wire fence. To get in and out I had to crawl, but a sheep could manage perfectly.

And now we had a field and an intake. The ewes had somewhere to lamb and the hoggs had a base from which to practise their moorcraft.

I decided that now I was in a position to apply for the government's hill sheep subsidy claimed by all my neighbours. I announced this at Jim's house where we were assembled to help with a Brucellosis test.

'I wish you luck,' said George and Jim. 'I don't think she

ought to get it,' said George's wife Sandra. 'If she does they'll all want it.'

If they'd worked as hard as I did, I thought, sinking my teeth into one of Flora's excellent bakewell tarts, they deserved it.

But I said nothing.

Foundlings

Six lengths of baler band, the hairy sisal sort, plaited for half their length, lay over my arm as I went to get Geraldine.

I could see her, all alone in Jim's reseeded intake, and my heart was heavy as I called to her and she careered down to see what I had brought for her. If she had known she would not have been so eager.

Since I have lived here, I have seen that intake change from an enclosure of heather and bilberries to a cornfield, a turnip field, and now at last to a meadow. And sheep shouldn't be in meadows, especially other people's.

Why Geraldine seemed to be the only one wicked enough to insist on entering the forbidden meadow I couldn't say, but she achieved it daily by leaping a moor wall that turned two hundred others. She didn't clear it cleanly, of course – four faults every time – but each assault on that wall meant a breach in the defences and the temptation to others to follow her example. If that meadow could remain unmolested it would become hay, and that hay would be needed to nourish, among many others, Geraldine and her first lamb, so it was only common sense that I should do my best to stop her.

I tried gapping up the obvious places in the stone wall, tying strange objects to the strandwire above it, taking her for long walks to 'lose' her higher up the moor, and tying a fancy eyeshade to her horns to blind her as she looked up at the forbidden wall. Wearing it, she made her best jump yet. I saw her.

So now it was the cross-band, and I stood with the dreadful thing in my hand and called her down to me, happy and trusting, to be handicapped with one of the hill shepherd's more severe forms of restraint. I was told that a week or so in a cross-band, under supervision, would 'break her heart'. Time would decide; but the decision to use it had already broken mine.

A cross-band is a kind of hobble, one hind leg is tied to the opposite foreleg by a rope a little shorter than the sheep's natural stride, so that she can graze, walk, even run, but not jump, since she cannot move both forelegs together.

All afternoon I experimented, shortening and lengthening the rope until I was sure it would do its job without unnecessary discomfort. I tied the ends carefully to avoid chafing her legs and by night I was sure that I had done all I could. I tried to even things up by removing the other handicap she wore – the fine, heavy fleece that would not be needed since she cannot go to the moor in her cross-band. At the back of my mind also was the thought that now I had done all the violence I intended her and could somehow try to make amends, for I loved her dearly.

She was the saddest little pet lamb I had ever reared. I first saw her lying in a pool of muddy water, too lame to do more than raise her pretty head to look at me. The soft earth around her bore evidence of her struggles to rise. She was covered in ticks, some of the old bites angry and infected, her joints swollen, her limbs useless.

So often lambs, like adult sheep, bow to the inevitability of their end in such circumstances. The light in their eyes goes out, they detach themselves and seem to go to meet their death. But this lamb spoke quite clearly through the eyes that glowed like jet beads in the dusk. She was not ready to die, she begged for a chance to live. I begged her to take that chance and she grasped it wholeheartedly.

The only practical help I could offer was a course of penicillin injections, a steady supply of goat milk and the loan of my legs to carry her where her own refused to go, to find grazing, shelter, sunshine and shade when I thought she needed them. Each morning I would set her on her legs and they would buckle like cold spaghetti and I would tuck her resolutely under my arm, asking 'where shall we graze today?'

It was a joint effort, this grazing business. I would settle her on her brisket in a nice level place and she would mow happily around her as far as her neck would reach, while I visited her from time to time with choice goodies and tasty finds from the pastures which I now saw through a sheep's sharp, hungry eyes.

I remember once finding an ash tree whose base was surrounded by new green shoots and the lush, acid green tempted me as though such things formed part of my own diet. Geraldine loved ash leaves.

She would lie patiently while I exercised her useless limbs and when the great day came and she tottered a few real steps, we all went wild with joy. The children organised a daft party for all the lambs, with flaked maize and weaner pellets and a lot of laughing and leaping about around the strange, patient little soul for whom recovery was, at last, in sight. Even so, if anyone had told me that this gently self-effacing creature would, within a twelve month, leap five-foot walls to become a thorn in the flesh of all and sundry, I should not have believed it.

All her contemporaries had settled on the moor but Geraldine – now technically a shearling – had returned home in disgrace for a course of mild correction. I watched her as she struggled with the awkward band, stumbling and stopping and learning to walk all over again as she did a year ago. I went home near to tears.

Later that night I called Snuff for her evening snack.

Down the hill she pounded, her lambs bouncing on all fours behind her and – lo and behold – Geraldine, trundling down with her to be sure she didn't miss anything. Moving awkwardly, I admit, as the measures were designed to ensure, but with no evidence of real distress. It worked.

She was quite unable to jump up on to the low wall where Snuff and the lambs ate, so I gave her a fistful of food of her own. I did remember, just for a moment, that she was supposed to be in disgrace, but I told myself that the purpose of the confinement of offenders is to reform rather than to punish, and slipped her another dairy nut.

Our Geraldine grew into a very big shearling indeed, and when I rounded up all the breeding sheep for their routine pre-lambing inoculations it was clear that she was building up a healthy supply of milk for the first lamb that was, by that time, only a couple of weeks away.

This was the last year I borrowed Jim's intake for the purpose, and lambing went ploddingly ahead. The old faithfuls lambed without difficulty, but I fidgeted and worried as time went on, my fingers perpetually crossed that the shearlings, the vulnerable first-timers, would manage as well. I watched them carefully and one day, as I was rounding up the latest arrival for a few squirts of marking fluid and an eartag, I spotted the unmistakable signs of impending parturition in the first of the shearlings – Geraldine.

She was a little apart from the others, restless, suspicious. She did not gallop up as usual but kept her distance and as the cheerful throng jostled against my knees in their single-minded desire to swallow one more ewe and lamb pencil than the next sheep, and the new, white thistledown lambs played king-of-the-castle on a moles' breeding-hill, Geraldine stood aloof, watching.

I went up again a little later, spying from a secret place, and she was still there, under the wall. I left her, resolving to come up again just before dark.

But when I finally arrived up at the intake, with everything fed and watered from pigs to lettuces, it was nearly dark that I had to walk up to the wall at the top to find her. What I saw when I got there was a little pile of stones dislodged by her pregnant clumsiness and a wisp of fresh wool caught up in the wire which fluttered forlornly in the miserable north-east wind. She had gone.

It never occurred to me that she might jump out. Leaving a field of good grass for the wild, barren moor. I stumbled up the rough track in the gathering darkness but it was no earthly use. I called, but I knew it was hopeless. Instinct had taken over and she was off to find the real seclusion that was, after all, her birthright. I knew there was precious little point in going on but I wandered among the heather until it was quite dark, and returned home desolate. Nancy asked whether she had had her lamb and I told her what had happened. She asked if it would be all right and I said that it probably would – after all, Geraldine is a big sheep and if she had enough wild instinct to drive her to the high places, chances were instinct would help her clean the lamb and mother it; but there still lurked at the back of my mind the nagging little doubt that she might not manage to lamb or might run away from her lamb or even, as sometimes happens with shearlings, love the lamb dearly, lick it and croon to it but refuse to let it suck so that it would quietly fade like a little flower, fold up and die. I didn't sleep very well.

I went out as soon as it was light. I knew that if Geraldine were in any trouble, I must find her in the next few hours. I set off from the same place she had done, and went straight up the rigg, searching walls and quiet hollows from Parci Gill to the peat bog and found several ewes and several lambs, but of Geraldine there was no sign. Nothing was amiss on that side of the moor it seemed, and I went back for a bit of breakfast feeling better. After all, if so many ewes brought forth their lambs way out of human ken, why should our Geraldine be any exception?

After a couple of cups of strong coffee I went up again, trying a different track. I hadn't gone very far, however, when I saw a still woollen figure on the edge of a patch of burned heather. I went closer. I saw that it was a neighbour's ewe and saw, and smelt, that all was not well with her. She lay still, her breath laboured, and behind her, dragging on the ground, lay the forequarters of a huge lamb, half-born and very dead. It stank.

I relieved the poor creature of her hideous burden, but could not leave her there. I heaved her up into my arms and trotted back down the moor with her. I left her in my own tiny field, and went to tell her owner, who gathered up an antibiotic injection and set off to try to save her. Again I set off in search of Geraldine.

I searched the grassy hills on the moor end, and gullies and scree-slopes above the old school, then set off along the back of the wall to Arnsgill. The wind had come round to the north-west and there was a sea-drizzle in it. Perhaps she had gone to shelter up there behind the wall. Again I saw ewes in plenty, and fine, strong lambs. But no Geraldine.

I turned to come home by the bigger track and stared around me until my eyes ached. I stopped at last on a strange, round, acid-green knoll that must have puzzled many a walker who does not know that once a lorry over-turned here with a load of lime. It is a strange little landmark. From it you can see the tip of Sunburnt Nab, across the river, the fields of Rye Farm and Head House, but of the moorland immediately around you can see almost nothing for the little hills that rise all around. I knew suddenly that I had come too far. After all, when Geraldine was a lamb I learned to think like a sheep as I grazed and foraged for her. Fool that I was, could I not think her way now? I knew that she would never come this far, nor would she seek safety in places that were way beyond her normal running.

I had heard that a ewe about to lamb could go miles, stray unpredictably. Instinct told her to go to a place where

73

she knew she would be safe. But Geraldine would, I was suddenly certain, choose somewhere familiar. I would have looked for her, at any other time, along the broad band of heather that lay now half way between me and home. I would look a little on my way back but the chances of finding anything in that great expanse of deep, ragged heather were almost negligible, and anyway time was running out. I would have to trust her.

I came upon her suddenly. I saw a sheep in the distance and I knew it was her. I called and ran as though she should have been as pleased to see me as I was her. I could see no lamb. She took a step or two towards me, then turned, looked and called. And there rose up from a hollow in the heather the biggest, best and bonniest lamb that was ever born on that wild old moor. I went a little closer.

What a beauty it was. A gimmer. It called crossly to its mother and she went to it, comforting it with her quiet voice and soft lips.

I knelt a long while in the heather until my knees were stiff, and then I went singing home again.

Not long after that another of the shearlings, June, gave birth to a fine strong tup lamb, but at a fortnight old he began to fail. I took both of them down to the fields near the house, and gradually he faded away. June fussed and fretted, finally keeping a sad vigil by his little body until I hunted up a frail and needy foster-lamb for her. We called him Pipsqueak and a poor, weedy little thing he was to be sure, feeling like a woollen toy that has been injudiciously put through a washing machine, limp in my arms as I carried him home. All the same, his dull little eyes shone beady-bright when I first introduced him to poor, bereaved June, and he dived in at once to make the most of his opportunity when I held her steady. Since her own lamb had died of no recognisable disease, I risked the age-old trick of putting poor little Pipsqueak into his predecessor's skin before I tried to foster him on, but he was so small I had to take tucks in here, there and everywhere and had to cut a big flap off the back so that it didn't trip him up as he trailed round the pen in dogged determination after the little sheep who had, as far as he was concerned, everything a little lamb could ever want.

We were winning, I know we were, and June's objections to Pipsqueak were being gradually worn down by his cheeky persistence and her own compelling need when tragedy struck again and poor June went suddenly blind and stood stupidly in one place, paddling from foot to foot, waiting, or so it seemed, for death to come and take her. I called the vet, whose prompt diagnosis and treatment saved her life, but her milk supply failed utterly.

Poor Pipsqueak just couldn't understand why the new mother he was coming to depend upon now failed him. She was too ill to make any effort at physical rejection but she stood sullen, unloving and dry while the little fellow crept beneath her, whimpering, acting out once again the tragedy that had brought him to this point. I took him into a shed and offered him a bottle of fresh goat milk, which he glugged without enthusiasm. He was afraid of me. A poor, woollen changeling, neither sheep nor child and I wanted to hug him hard, but it seemed as if the little twig legs would crumble to dust in their slack covering of dry, fuzzy wool. When I went to offer him a second bottle, later in the day, he turned his head away, curled back his top lip and moaned faintly. He could not stand.

His belly felt hard and tight, the area beneath his tail a little too clean and a little too dry. As far as I could make out, what with so many changes of milk and mothers, his insides had gone on strike, and there was no earthly use trying to force more food down unless I could ensure that it continued its journey in nature's planned manner. I hesitated to use a purgative on something so very frail, but I had no way of knowing that he had fed properly during his first twenty-four hours, no way of telling for sure whether he had ever managed to rid himself of the protective contents of his tiny gut as in the normal way of newborn things. I pondered.

The vet had just left again, shaking his head sadly and preparing me for the worst after seeing my little pet pig, Petal. I was going to have a sleepless night as I couldn't leave her to die in pain with a bowel oedema – but what if I did something similar to poor Pipsqueak. It seemed as if this run of bad luck had set in forever.

I set up an intensive care ward, with the syringe of pain-killer the vet had left me lying beside the peaceful pig and very carefully I administered a tiny dose of liquid paraffin to Pipsqueak, and as he swallowed hard, just the once, I prayed that I had not signed his death warrant.

It was a very long night. When Petal woke and suffered I used up the medication, and when she woke again and suffered again and I knew it was all hopeless, I killed her painlessly, and after she had gone I hurt inside so very badly that I almost resented the miserable Pipsqueak and his bleating presence, hardly doing more than remark to myself that the dose appeared to be having some effect.

On and off, all night long, Pipsqueak rid himself systematically of the accumulated contents of his long-suffering insides and somehow, when morning finally came, I was sitting, still fully dressed, beside the poor little pig, rocking sorrowfully backwards and forwards with Pipsqueak in my arms. He felt like a skeleton – a balsa-wood skeleton – but he was alive. Just. When I stirred he bumbled his fuzzy lips against my earlobe. He was hungry.

The spring days slipped by. Googie the goat produced two fine nanny kids and came into full production, and the nursery was full of bouncing babies with Pipsqueak among the bounciest, first for his bottle, bounding up into my arms, a cupboard-loving, quivering desire for warm sweet milk. When I went to feed him he turned his bright beady eyes up to me and sucked and nuzzled under my chin with a desperation that would have convinced anyone who did not know he had been fed only a couple of hours earlier.

Just as I had begun to believe that the run of bad luck had ended, it struck again. I went up to the moor to see whether Geraldine had got back her baby. Young Heather, of whose birth I told you, had been missing when I went up to see them all that morning and I was uneasy. Geraldine's udder felt a little lumpy and she hadn't been suckled for a few hours, but I told myself not to worry. Heather would be lying asleep in her own fragrant, woody element, and I would see her at dusk. Nothing would be wrong, I told myself, but the cold rock in the pit of my stomach was preparing me all along for the possibility of disaster.

I found Heather in a little grassy gully not far up the moor. Her body was blown up like a balloon, her skin, where it showed through the wool, grey-green. There was stained foam in her nostrils and she was horribly dead. Pride, they say, always goes before a fall, and I was prouder of Heather than of any of the others. It looked like pulpy kidney disease and I couldn't believe it. All the sheep had been carefully inoculated and there had recently been a change of pasture, not from poor to lush but the other way round. She was a fine thriving lamb, sure enough, but the chances of her dying like that in the circumstances in which she had been kept seemed remote indeed. I could hardly bear it. Sympathetic fellow farmers told me it was a chance in a million; but did I have to be the one to fall victim to that chance? I walked on up the moor after I found her, wallowing in self-pity. One of the others could have been taken, surely, and not the loveliest of them all. One lamb had to be the one in a million that could not be saved, but did it have to be mine? Not again. Not Heather.

I saw Geraldine trotting hopefully back to the still body and I caught her and took her home. I dared not let her go for fear she developed mastitis and turned up at clipping time ruined and in agony like one of my first sheep. I had nowhere to pen her. Nowhere except . . .

I put her in with the little lamb, who greeted her joyful and trusting. Was this the mother he had sought so long? Was it all going to be for the best even if it were second-best? It was worth a try. 'Pipsqueak', I told him, 'This is Geraldine'.

By the following spring Pipsqueak had grown into a fine, yearling tup. He still lived with us because, as an entire male, he would have threatened the virtue of the female yearlings on the moor. He lived with another lamb, growing up side by side with Doris, Googie the goat's daughter. It was in early March that the accident happened.

Any parent of a toddler knows what it's like. You're all ready to do something – a trip, a visit, anything – and then comes the little tug of the sleeve, the urgent whisper. And so much of life's frustration crystallises into that admonishing undertone – 'couldn't you have gone while you had the chance?'

Anyone who has ever been in the position of seeking an urgently needed facility with an anxious fidgeting youngster in tow will know how I felt about our Doris.

She had every chance of mating with a very able billy goat, blast her, so why should she suddenly decide, in the middle of Sunday dinner, that she wanted a billy and wanted him NOW!?

At first I couldn't believe it but as I watched and listened I knew there was no way I could be mistaken. Our Doris was in season. A nanny goat's bleat is not a lovely sound at the best of times, but the voice of a nanny in season has an edge of tetchiness that is quite distinctive and this, coupled with the fanning of the tail and extraordinary insistence on accompanying me everywhere, left no room for doubt. Little Doris had grown up, not with a bang but with a monotonous, wailing bleat.

I went to ring a friend with a billy goat. We had already sold ours. Henry's owners were going out, but he would be happy to oblige the following day. I went home and told

Doris, who wailed louder. I told her to make the best of it and started the evening feed-round. She followed me steadfastly.

I filled up the haynets in the goat shed, hoping she'd stay in and eat, but she wouldn't look at her good food. I filled the trough, but nuts were not to her liking.

I took another scoop of nuts from the bin and went on to the next group of hungry creatures, all fastened in another shed. Blue, the wether, almost ready for a friend's freezer, and Pipsqueak.

I went into the building and Doris followed. I saw a glance pass between her and Pipsqueak and then, before I had time to register what was happening let alone do anything about it, the pair had come to a decision of their own and were demonstrating their commitment with all the gusto one associates with young, healthy creatures.

As soon as was practicable, I separated the pair, isolating Doris outside Pipsqueak's chainlink fence, but any damage was now, presumably, done and the starcrossed lovers kissed and muttered excitedly through the mesh.

Jim came by and I told him what had happened. His reply was brief and to the point, his disbelief quite evident. So I let Pipsqueak out and the whole joyous madcap game began again. I had got over my initial horror at this intermarriage of species and called my daughter to see.

For five and a half hours Pipsqueak pursued his boisterous courtship and I knew that Henry's chances were now nil. I wondered about possible issue from the union – after all, folk tales of such matings are rife. Only this summer a local dealer told me in Northallerton Mart that he had bought just such a creature and, although I didn't believe him at the time, wondered now.

Before bed, I separated the satiated Juliet from her exhausted Romeo. All night I dreamed of fabulous beasts, of providing, at last, a documented account of such an unlikely coupling and its outcome.

In the morning, though, I telephoned our beloved vet, whom God preserve, of Northallerton, and he said that because of a discrepancy in the number of chromosomes in the genetic blueprint of the two species, Doris could never carry Pipsqueak's scions. I must say I felt rather sad about that.

Still, this being so, Doris would come in season again in a few weeks, and I resolved to lock her in some ivory tower until I could get her to Henry. But it would have been nice . . . I reported that incident in my newpaper column, and received a letter from a reader who was deeply offended at my frankness as to the escapade. I apologised for having caused the offence, but not for writing the article. All the same I thought seriously before including it in a book. But it was true, every word of it, and if you had been there and felt the joyous exuberance of two fit young animals, I don't think you would have felt in the least uneasy.

Sex is. Reproduction happens. Shakespeare referred to such subjects as 'country matters' and in nature there are few artificial inhibitions. The person who voiced the objection is a country person. How much greater, then, the chances that I have offended my town readers. If I have done so, it is because I failed to convey the joy, the innocence, the openness of the event as it actually happened, and that, for a writer, is failure indeed, and I am very sorry. I'll do better next time!

That, incidentally, was one of the events that did occur in a somewhat bleak week – a repeat of the aforementioned incident which took me quite unawares. You see, my arithmetic was very shaky and I had expected Doris's return to service a week later than it actually occurred – you see, even my livestock husbandry is sometimes of a low standard!

So to make sure next time, I borrowed an ugly little brown billy goat and sent Pipsqueak out to the moor with his Swaledale cousins. Next autumn he would serve in the capacity of tup, but meanwhile we looked only to the next step on the long ladder to spring and the joyous surprise-party of another lambing time.

For the lambs still come, you know, even though no storks have been sighted in the National Park for many years.

Pipsqueak as a baby (author's photo)

Swine Fever

They came at last. Rosalie Pig, keeping us all on tenterhooks till the last possible moment, gave birth to 11 strong piglets and all the long last days of waiting were made worthwhile as one by one the little strangers slid forth into the world, blinked, squealed, then trundled doggedly round underneath the dear sow's uplifted hind leg to connect up unerringly to the main milk supply.

I didn't go in. I watched, with modified breathing that made my chest ache, over the top of the door for a while and it was obvious that Rosalie had everything well under control. Good old pig, settling sensibly to the job in hand, she grunted as she worked and her soft, gentle voice seemed to draw the little pigs forward to their source of comfort as surely as the outstretched arms of a human mother.

One hundred and eighteen days it took her, from the visit of the boar to the achievement of 11 suckling pigs and my fine, modern pig-husbandry book was proved wrong again. I don't know why I bother with it anyway, since it begins one chapter with the words 'No-one could describe the pig as being an intelligent or affectionate animal.'

I could, for one. I do. I can only assume that for anyone to be able to put into practice some of the disgusting theories propounded in the book one would have to convince oneself that pigs were devoid of all feeling, and the end result of such atrocities as cage rearing and the fastening of hundreds of sows in tiny cubicles, day in, day out, would have to be, I suppose, a creature somewhat lacking in the normal emotional development of its species. But then, I'm one of those who find factory farming the most sickening result of the universal greed which enforces the necessity of employing less and less stockmen to attend more and more creatures, and I happen to be rather fond of pigs, especially Rosalie.

But this was not a day for the grinding of axes, rather for the celebration of the successful conclusion of a four-month joint enterprise and the twins clamoured for news every time I came in from one of my trips to sty or barn.

For in the barn slept old Snuff, weary with the weight of the lamb she had carried almost to the end of its journey and I knew from her changed behaviour that her time, too, was not far off.

I flashed the torch into the darkness of the barn and her one good eye shone green. Her jaws worked rhythmically and I knew that she was not quite ready yet. Rosalie had won.

'Eleven pigs,' I told the twins. 'A football team!' 'Let's call them Pigs United!' They were so very thrilled. I would have been a spoilsport to point out that we mustn't congratulate ourselves too soon, that little pigs are very vulnerable and that the weather had turned very, very cold. I secretly wished that the book had been right, and that she had farrowed earlier, during the warm dry days of the week before. The only heat I could manage was a hurricane lamp hung on a nail, but the sty is stone-built and warm and it was well-bedded and insulated. It felt cosy when I went in to check that all was well before I made my final visit to Snuff and went happily to bed.

Next morning there were still 11 pigs. They had survived their first night and I was delighted.

All the next day I stayed close to the house, and to Snuff and Rosalie, carrying buckets of warm pig-gruel, choice handfuls of hay, pignuts and sheepnuts and buckets of water. I stayed up till the small hours and when I went for my last check a white frost gripped everything and the sharp cold made me catch my breath. Still no lamb, and I made a curtain of meal-bags for the gap at the top of the sty door.

At four in the morning I was up again to check Snuff. No lamb. I went to the pigs' door and then changed my mind. All was silence and I decided it would be better not to let a blast of icy air into the sty. I hurried back indoors and crept into bed for another few hours' sleep.

Soon after six, I woke again and went out on another reconnaissance mission. Snuff still had not lambed and I made Rosalie's breakfast. She got up when I came in and trotted to her trough. The pyramid of piglets in the corner squeaked into life and the upper layers pottered out of the nest to find their mother's dung-piles and add their own little contributions.

The three piglets at the bottom of the heap did not move. They lay horribly still, and there was a dark empty space of ages between seeing them and realising they must be dead. I picked them up and they were limp and hot. I stuffed them inside my anorak and ran into the house. Somehow I didn't want Rosalie to see. I rubbed and blew and administered whisky and two of them flickered back to life. I returned them to Rosalie who was feeding the rest and she grunted them up as though she were scolding them for coming late to table.

But I wasn't amused. In the house, beside the bedroom fire, lay a fine, silk-skinned piglet, her eyes shut, her small face smiling, in a sleep that was forever. Pigs United could now field only ten men and my cardboard smile lasted just long enough to see the twins off to school before I allowed myself a cry for the little life I might have saved if only I had gone in and got them all on their feet before I went back to bed.

With the twins at school I was alone with my misery, so I went to the barn and thought aloud as I tended old Snuff. I settled myself beside her and buried my face in the great ruff of springy wool round her neck. She, in turn, swung her coal-black head on to my shoulder. I could feel her strong jaws chewing, chewing, and it had the effect of a comforting massage.

Not many people, perhaps, would describe the sheep as being an intelligent or affectionate animal. But I would.

The pain passed, as such pain must. We turned to the bringing up of the remaining ten pigs, which proved to be all female but one. Ascertaining that, however, was something of a major operation, demanding careful forethought, military precision of manoeuvre, and nerves of steel. Pigs, you must understand, never do anything by halves, and from the moment they can totter about, piglets are either galloping full tilt into some kind of mischief or sound asleep, the only sign of life being the occasional gusty sigh. To touch them at this stage, though, galvanises the whole heap into instant activity and off they go again, hell for leather, into the wild blue yonder. To attempt to handle them with Rosalie anywhere near would be to invite trouble. Rosalie resents any interference with the youngsters that causes them distress, and they, playing this up for all they are worth, will squeal piteously if their feet are lifted off the ground, bringing the old sow at the gallop, ears akimbo, ready to take on all comers in mortal combat.

So, how did I go about it? Well for a start, I let Rosalie out of the sty and gave her a heap of potatoes to munch. Then I locked the door, which can only be done from the outside, leaving me to climb over the top of the chainlink fence carrying a large apple box. Into this, one by one, went the piggies – gilt after gilt after gilt. Once they were in the box they were quiet because nobody was handling them, but they were restrained from squirting all over the sty like pieces of wet soap and being counted twice or three times each, a circumstance which had hitherto convulsed the issue. There was definitely only one little boar pig. Good. It wouldn't be much of a job to divest him of his 'belongings', which would have to be done soon to prevent taints in the meat.

Meat. A sobering thought. But as the terrible ten whizzed madly across a field to the nearest wallow-hole, scattering all before them in their madcap progress, I was reminded of a letter I received from a reader who regretted that so many of this exploited species never have, as he put it, a decent run for their limited lives. These pigs would have just that until it was time to part. Right now they were lying in a filthy heap, mud from top to trotters, in an exhausted sleep, with here and there a small snout, washed pink again in the food-trough, from which issued now and then a sleepy grunt.

The little boar pig, though, caused me much deliberation. Ernest, the first pig we ever had, happened to be a little lad, and the avid reading of books that accompanied the acquisition of any new kind of creature left me in no doubt that unless he was intended for use as a stud boar, he should be divested as soon as possible of his masculinity in order that his carcase should not be tainted and made unacceptable. I couldn't imagine any aspect of Ernest being unacceptable to anybody, but the books were adamant that all young male pigs should be castrated and the books were all I had to protect my pig from my ignorance. I asked my neighbours whether they would help me and each man I approached suggested another so sincerely as being 'a good hand' that I began to suspect that the cutting of pigs must be a rural skill of unfathomable complexity. When at last a kind little man from the top of the dale arrived, highly recommended by everyone else, with his tall son and a little bottle of iodine, I was shaking as I went out to meet him.

I called Ernest. He sped into the yard. The son caught him and held him aloft upside down. With the breaking of the contact between his feet and the ground he set up the ear-splitting squeal we had come to associate with any such assault on his person. I knew from experience that it would continue until foursquare contact with terra firma was re-established.

What, I wondered, would he do when the operation actually began. I steeled myself. I saw the little man produce a scalpel, make two small holes in the scrotum, withdraw the testicles, sever them, drop them, dab the wounds with iodine, and signal his son to put Ernest down again, and all in less time than it took to tell it. During that time the pig's squeals did not change, and when he found himself upright again he trundled off quite happily, pausing only to swallow the two tasty morsels he found alongside his deflowerer's boots. So much for mystery.

When Rosalie's first litter came, the problem arose again, six times beneath three of the eight tails. Although I was not quite so apprehensive as before, I still sent the same plaintive cry circulating – 'who will cut my pigs?' This time there was Alice, who had moved with her family to a big farm across the river. She offered to send her husband, Derek, who was she assured me 'a good hand'. This time I was to hold the pigs.

Alice and Derek, sadly, no longer live in the dale, but we still meet from time to time, and when we do, reference is always made to the day we cut the pigs.

I caught and upended the first victim, just as had been done to Ernest. I froze my face into studied immobility and steeled myself. With painful slowness Derek laid out his implements and made ready to begin. Then, just as he was about to make the first incision, he said brightly 'It's twenty years since I cut a pig. Now, what do I do first . . .' I couldn't see the ruination of my carefully composed expression, but Alice could, and her description of my silent panic has been repeated over many a cup of tea. That was my first introduction to Derek's sense of humour and probably the origin of my first grey hair.

And now there was another boar pig approaching the age of no return, and I was faced again with the same difficulty.

Twice I had observed the operation. There was a page of glossy photographs in my pig-book that gave step-by-step instructions. I could do it. All I needed was someone to hold the pig.

I prevailed upon my neighbour, Jim, to oblige, and he agreed to lend me both his strength and his scalpel. When he turned up to do the job, I saw with mixed feelings that he had also brought his wife. As soon as she was within earshot I heard her say, 'I don't think she should do it,' and I felt sure that she had been making that point all the way along the lane. What little confidence I had mustered shrivelled to a tiger-nut. But, shaking hands notwithstanding, I made two tiny cuts, withdrew two tiny testicles, and sprayed the little wounds with antiseptic as though I did such things every day. It was only when I tried to resume cheerful conversation and found that my voice was constricted by an excruciating pain in my chest that I realised I had not allowed myself to breathe during the operation. But I had done it. With a little more practice, I told myself, I would be 'a good hand'.

The next litter was extraordinary in that, of twelve little pigs, ten were boars. This, I felt sure, was to lead to my finest hour. Already people were expressing surprise and admiration that I had been able to manage this rather alarming task. I glowed. I quite looked forward to the day when my neighbour (and his wife) would come to assist (and observe). I'd show them expertise in action!

But pride, as always, goes before a fall, and the fall, when it came, was shattering.

With so many pigs to cut, it was necessary to make special arrangements to contain old Rosalie, who becomes understandably upset when she thinks her babies are being interfered with. By the time my neighbours arrived I had separated her from the piglets and cornered them up in the sty. I began well. Three done and seven to go.

The fourth little pig felt different, but no alarm bells rang.

'He's only got one,' I commented cheerfully. I had had experience of lambs with only one testicle and wasn't unduly worried. I thought I could feel the missing article a little higher up, and all, I felt sure, would be revealed once I had made my incision. Just how right that assumption proved to be I was to find out.

I had heard of ruptured boars, of course, during occasional piggy conversations with fellow enthusiasts, but I had no idea of what this meant in purely practical terms. I made my incision.

What happened next can only have taken a split second, yet it is recorded on my memory in graphic slow motion. The tissues beneath the blade swelled out and the last papery layer of skin split and parted. And out came the larger part of the poor little animal's lower gut. Coil upon coil of warm, livid plumbing, as though his inside were knitted in wet wool and was being unravelled yard by crinkled yard. 'Now you've done it' said my laconic assistant.

'What are you going to do now,' shrieked his wife. And, incredibly, I knew just what I was going to do. An icy calm overtook me. I caught the warm, pulsating gut in the palm of my left hand, opened the lips of the wound with the fingers of my right, and stuffed it all back in again. Then I nipped the edges of the wound together. 'Can you hold him?' I asked my neighbour, over the earsplitting shrieks. He nodded. I turned to his wife, 'Hold that', and ran off into the house. In the bathroom, on the shelf, was a spool of nylon fishing line. I would thread a needle with it and sew up the little pig; sew back all the wet, red ruin of his inside; never lay eyes on it again . . . My fingers found the spool. I would have to go back downstairs, find a needle, thread it – but I was rooted to the spot, peering out of the bathroom window at the pigsty, where the shrieks of the suspended piglet ripped the warm, pungent air, and Rosalie, her mother's instincts roused to fever pitch, tore with her great teeth at the chainlink fence that separated her from the scene of the assault on her young ones. I knew that inside that building my neighbour stood holding the ruined pig, and his wife like the little boy with his finger in the dyke stood with her knuckles whitening, preventing him from turning wholly inside-out. And the strangest thought crossed my mind. What if I were not to go back? What if I just disappeared, left them to it, stuck like the peasants to the golden goose? And a weird sound rang out, echoing off the bathroom tiles. It was laughter. The most terrible thing I could remember having done and I was laughing like a drain! It was hysteria, and I pulled myself together and went for a needle.

I sprayed a great pool of purple antibiotic into the interior of the piglet and did a textbook mattress suture. I injected him with a generous dose of penicillin and put him back in the straw. Then I lifted the next pig by one hind leg, handed it to my neighbour, took up the scalpel and castrated it neatly. And that was far harder to do than the emergency repair of a moment previously.

I rang the vet. He said it was extremely unlikely that the piglet would live. I had done my best to avoid infection, but shock would probably kill him before any infection had a chance to develop. I wept then, and shook with all the fright that had mercifully waited to afflict me until after I had taken what action I could to remedy my own tragic error.

Two things followed that are especially worthy of note. One was the amazing survival of the little pig, who was sold with the rest of the litter at ten weeks old. The other was something one of the market drovers said as I went to the office to collect the money. I had told him the story of the miraculous pig, and he said in a conversational sort of way that nobody cuts pigs any more. They got them to pork weight so quickly now that it doesn't matter. And sure enough, all the other litters I've sold since have had their boars left entire.

Yet another of my newly acquired skills had become obsolete, it appeared – just as I was getting to be a good hand. But I can't say I was as upset as usual by the discovery.

It was after the weaning of that litter that I detected a lump above one of Rosalie's teats and asked the vet's advice about treatment for mastitis. He prescribed a course of antibiotic injections. So far so good.

But Rosalie was no longer the same little pig to whom I administered tetanus anti-toxin a couple of years before. She was now a very big sow indeed and I asked for his advice on how and where she should be injected.

He said in serious tones that while one can specify with smaller creatures that substances should be introduced sub-cutaneously, or as intravenous or intramuscular jabs, when one is dealing with such a creature as Rosalie one can but strive to ensure that it ends up intra-pig. I saw what he meant.

However, nothing daunted, I loaded my trusty syringe and set forth to do battle with the great barrage balloon of a pig who was happily guzzling her meal in the yard, unaware of my unpleasant intentions.

Now what the vet had advised me to do seemed like as near perfect a technique as man has yet devised for getting potions into pigs, so I followed his directions to the letter.

I sidled up beside Rosalie and began to scratch affectionately at her left ear, with my left hand, then with the swiftness of a card-sharp I plonked the sharp end of the syringe, which I was holding firmly against my thumb into the little flat behind her right one. And then I found the flaw in the plan. I had nothing left with which to press the plunger!

Not long before this, I had been told by a young CB radio enthusiast that pigs were known, in the special cant of the 'breaker' as go-go dancers. When I was first told this, I couldn't believe it. I couldn't see what such a description had to do with such calm and sensible creatures. Now I knew, and I can say with reasonable certainty that whoever dreamed up that description has at some time or another attempted to administer some medication by injection intra-pig.

Like one of those loose-limbed ladies on TV she whirled, she gyrated and she flogged the syringe time and time again from my fumbling fingers with her great leathery ears. We covered a great deal of ground in one session when I was attempting to re-connect the barrel of the syringe to the needle which was stuck behind her ear like a tramp's dog-end.

In the end I managed to get the prescribed quantity into her carcase, parking the odd cubic centimetre into whatever part presented itself as and when I could; but I must confess that almost as much of the stuff ended up extra-pig one way and another.

I made a note to ask the vet whether, should the situation arise again, I might be better advised to make the stuff into an omelette and get it down that way.

We still have Rosalie, and I am still learning, although she is getting on a bit for a sow. Neighbours had begun to drop hints that I ought to be 'letting her go', as the euphemism has it. In other words, sending her to be slaughtered for fear her advancing age should lower her productivity, or in the most extreme view, ensuring that she died in the possession of someone else.

I become very defensive about things like this in connection with people like Rosalie. I went around for ages brandishing a picture from the *British Farmer and Stockbreeder* showing a Gloucester Old Spot the image of Rosalie, who was happily pregnant with her twentieth litter.

As far as I could see there was only one difference between Rosalie and this great monument to motherhood – and that was in the matter of front feet. The sow in the picture had little trotters that seemed fit to twinkle daintily to the trough until she was finally summoned to the great piggery in the sky. Rosalie's, by comparison, were overgrown and clumsy. They needed a trim, that's all, I told myself. And I got out all my pig books.

Not one of them so much as mentioned feet, except to say that good feet were essential to a good sow. Obvious. But the books seemed to be assuming, like everyone else, that the first signs of wear, be it teats or toenails, should be the signal for immediate dismissal from service. Not so, say I.

I asked friends who support this view, but none of them had ever had to trim a sow's feet. I have trimmed dog's nails, sheep feet, pony hooves, but my experience didn't stretch to pigs, so I phoned our beloved vet from Northallerton.

The problem, you see, was that Rosalie wouldn't necessarily be thrilled with the idea of having her nails done, and at thirty-odd stone it would be quite beyond my physical powers to persuade her otherwise. He reassured me at once, radiating confidence in me and my abilities. 'You can do it yourself,' he said, and I glowed. He prescribed something that would 'knock her out' and I set about gathering up tools. I mustered a pair of footrot shears, a small pair of wirecutters, and a huge pair of blacksmith's pincers which, I was assured, would do the job admirably.

I administered the knockout dose. Not in itself an easy task. The first few ccs went somewhat astray because the hypodermic needle gave up the unequal struggle against the horny hide, but I succeeded in the end in getting enough of the tranquilliser into the old lady to produce a satisfying jelly-legged euphoria, and I withdrew discreetly until it took its full effect. But how would I know?

I listened outside the sty until there was no sound but deep piggy breathing and then tiptoed to the door. In my mind's eye I could see her, lying on her side, legs outstretched, sighing contentedly, just as when she nursed her young ones. I held tight to my tools and took a deep breath.

Rosalie just hadn't bothered to read the stage directions. There she was all right, apparently dead to the world and snoring most single-mindedly, but not lying on her side as I had envisaged. No, she was lying on her belly, with her whiskery snout stretched forward into the clean straw, sniffing the odours of summertime and wheatfields, dreaming of happy things, judging by the smile that lifted the corners of her lips and, to my horror, all four trotters tucked tidily out of sight under the whole of that great bulk!

With bated breath I groped underneath and hooked my fingers behind one fat little knee. She opened both eyes as wide as possible for a pig and barked, just the once, in an obvious pig-equivalent of a four-letter word. I dropped the leg and fled. The medication I told myself, needed more time, which I could assuredly use to great profit by re-thinking my plan of campaign.

I was always told as a child, whenever I complained that I simply couldn't because the chisel was blunt, the screwdriver was broken or the fork was bent, that the bad workman always blames his tools.

I usually retaliated by saying that if they were anything like the sorry efforts I was forced to operate with, I didn't blame him. I don't suppose Rembrandt's brushes were ever reduced to a couple of bent whiskers or Grinling Gibbons' gouges ever as blunt as a bear's behind because someone had used them for opening baked bean tins. Put another way, the worst workman in the world can be lifted above his natural level of hopelessness by the chance to operate with the best possible apparatus.

And put yet another way, I would have been in a much better position to cope with the trimming of Rosalie Pig's trotters if only I had at my disposal something which would actually cut the stuff of which they are made. As it was, the position in which I found myself left much to be desired.

I was kneeling in the straw beside the somnolent form of the great pig like Red Riding Hood beside what purported to be her Granny. I was scratching the great leather lugs with my left hand, while with my right I tentatively groped beneath her bulk for the little fat front legs upon which she had comfortably collapsed. On the ends of those legs were the overgrown trotters to the trimming of which I now diligently applied myself. She was under the influence of a sedative from the vet, but I hadn't thought to ask him how long it would last, and there was an air of urgency about the operation, just in case.

The old girl was apparently unaware of everything. Her eyes were shut, and her breathing regular, lifting the slack upper lip at intervals to show the great fangs.

Again and again I fished for those feet. I could feel the tight little bend of her stubby knee and I heaved and pushed with all my might to lift her great weight off it so that I could straighten it and extend the leg out in front of her. It was the best I could do. There was no question of heaving her right over on her side in the position I had envisaged. I fiddled like a mechanic under a juggernaut.

During the manoeuvres it became clear that, while sedated, she was still vaguely aware of what was going on in her immediate vicinity. Time after time I would pull the great beast into a manageable position and just as I straightened the leg she would snore, stop, then bark out the piggy equivalent of 'go away – I've got a headache' and settle herself once more with her trotters pressed tight under her.

For hours, it seemed, I sat beside her, pleading, cajoling, begging, crying, despairing. If anyone had peered in it would have looked as if I were attempting to give the kiss of life to a beached whale.

Once or twice I succeeded in getting the leg stretched out and the pig undisturbed, but that left the trotter itself only inches from the somnolent snout with its great fangs and meant that I could feel her hot breath on the back of my hand as I tried to juggle the jaws of the mighty pincers into position.

But those great blacksmiths' pincers had as much effect on her rubbery old feet as a pair of kiddies' cutting-out scissors, and the ancient footrot shears I was lent 'in case' were about as effective as a chocolate teapot. In the end I nibbled off the edges painfully slowly with the funny little pliers that I use for getting wayward nails out of the soles of shoes. It wasn't the perfect job I'd envisaged and I felt desperately sad as I gathered up my useless implements then left the pig in peace.

So when I went shopping I went into my favourite hardware shop and fiddled about with a display of pruning shears for so long that a worried lady came and asked 'Can I help you?' I was dreading that. It put me in the position of having to explain that I was seeking the most suitable instrument for cutting the feet of pigs. 'Don't laugh,' I insisted. 'It isn't funny.'

Then suddenly I realised that it was funny. Very funny indeed. And in an atmosphere of high glee I selected a pair of Japanese secateurs that seemed to have been designed for the job. Fiendish clever, these orientals.

Rosalie pig looks through the door (author's photo)

Getting Away From It All

Before I wrote that first book and was drawn further from my hiding-place than I had ever imagined I would go, the occasions on which I ventured forth to do anything out of the ordinary were few and far between.

On the rare occasions I leave my perch in the Hambletons for the gentler landscape of the lower-down, I always visualise myself, in the few days before the excursion, sweeping down like an eagle to snatch the few titbits not available near at hand and soaring back triumphant.

The reality always falls short of these imaginings and the day we went to York to buy school uniform for my elder son was no exception.

It was no eagle but a somewhat unbalanced hen that fussed and fidgeted three children, three visitors and their baby into a Ford Zephyr which, though not vintage, could justifiably be called mature and whose working parts, like mine, showed signs of strain.

With little Kate's pushchair in the boot and a generous supply of jellytots aboard to quell mutiny, we blasted off an hour or so later than we had intended and our entry into civilisation coincided neatly with lunchtime closing.

Despite the fact that his gravy was probably cooling round the edges, our long-suffering local tradesman got as far as opening his till drawer to cash a cheque I had received, only to close it again as he noticed that it bore no signature. I left, penniless and covered in confusion to rejoin the rest of the crew who were covered in jellytots in varying stages of dissolution as baby Kate shared them generously with her cousins.

The mission hovered on the brink of abortion while wallets were searched for the wherewithal to continue.

It rained steadily. The children bickered. I withdrew to the only retreat available and slept until we reached York.

When Dick Turpin rode into York at the end of his journey, he could not have been more grateful than I was to be back on terra firma. I don't suppose he had to steer Black Bess under a little stripey pole like the one that swung up automatically to let us into the long-stay car park, but the grime and lather of his marathon ride would have been easier to get rid of than the remains of those jellytots, bits of which sparkled in Nancy's hair and clung with sugary determination to the more personal parts of the anatomy of those of us who had been sitting in the back seat.

The children wanted to see the pole working again, but there were no other cars about and when we pointed out that to operate it ourselves would cost us 15p, they said no more.

We set off bravely for the school outfitters and almost at once I began to see that their hours of walking about over heather and fields, their long trails along winding roads and their occasional marathon climbs over the hills, just to see what lay over the top, had done nothing to prepare them for walking across the city.

Almost at once one of them set off hell for leather to get a better look at the river, another fell behind to stare into someone's garden the third set off at a great pace, wheeling the pushchair as though heading for a free pie-and-pea supper some five miles away.

I stood still and bellowed for them all to return to base for instructions and my voice rang like a gong and strangers stopped momentarily and stared before hurrying out of range.

We continued on our way and my concentration began to make my head ache as we wove our way towards the city centre. In and out of the crowd they bobbed, now you see 'em, now you don't, and I was reminded of gathering sheep out of the brackens on the moor bottom. Seeing them forging steadily ahead, I took advantage of a slight break in the hideous and hitherto constant traffic to slip across the road, because I had seen an interesting shop. A yell from my sister-in-law told me that one of them had broken back from the main flock and innocently attempted to join me. I felt my grey hairs multiply.

At home, every evening, a black beetle makes his way across the carpet in the sitting room. He weaves in a rough diagonal, rushing over the light-coloured parts and stopping for breath on the dark bits of pattern. I watch him from far above, wondering about the nature of his beetlish business. So I must have appeared to any watcher from a height.

People milled about, brushing past without actual bodily contact, flowing in a great wave, utterly absorbed and intent upon each only knew what. I thought of the wood ants in the heap by the old lime kiln. If the watcher had dropped a giant bluebell among us all, would we have swarmed over it, stinging it until it went pink, scurrying as though we had been stirred with a stick? My head continued to ache.

Once when we were shopping in the village my sister-in-law had complained that she could not keep up with the speed of my walk and asked if such haste were necessary. My brother had soothed her with the assertion that after so many years of toiling up and down hills, it was only natural that I should go like the clappers of hell when set down on the flat. Here, though, I was unable to work up a decent stride, what with hopping and dodging like a prize-fighter, and my frustration grew to an unprecedented pitch as I saw

Nancy's red cape horribly far ahead and as unattainable as last Christmas.

I had a clear picture of what I should do – get the whole bunch up together and run off all the strangers like 'foreign' sheep against the nearest wall until I had separated what was mine from the mêlée. The frustration grew to anger as we crossed the road in little job-lots and the car that had semi-stopped to let me across nudged forward in little jerks like a cheat in a 100-yard sprint. I smiled sweetly at the driver and told him that I hoped he would stall at the next set of lights.

By this time my headache was so massive that I was peering through it like a naturalist in a hide and I wanted to go home.

I slept in the car. The merciful sleep of the dentist's chair. When I awoke it was all better. We bowled down the track to the house and my head cleared like magic in the sweet relief of safe return. I even laughed at my visitors' confusion as they dodged among the goats and poultry mustered in the yard. They looked so very out-of-place.

Now and again people ask me what we do to amuse ourselves up here in the hill. Casual visitors suggest that the days must blend together in a sort of sameness that would try the patience of a saint and drive a sinner to drink. Little do they know. More often than not, something that starts out as a perfectly average day can blossom into a full-scale event at the drop of my woolly hat.

On the second day of the school holidays, for instance, it became apparent that we would not survive into the third unless we somehow supplemented the contents of the kitchen cupboard.

We discussed possibilities. I could cycle to the village, but this might take up most of the day. Encumbered by the boneshaker, I could not accept a lift from anyone, and I would be limited in the amount I could bring home by the capacity of the basket. Andrew could go, but it would be beneath his dignity to ride on my district-nurse machine and his bike doesn't even have a basket. I could hitch-hike, as I often do, but three's a crowd to leave behind, and I thought one of them might like to come with me. But when I asked which of them would like to come the answer was unanimous – 'me'. So they all three came with me up the road and we waited for fate to send our transport.

The road was deserted apart from Old Henry and his dog. All our goats were in happy mischief in a field of clover fog, so we all waded in after them and dragged them all back, with much wailing and gnashing of teeth on both sides, to where they should have been. We returned to the road to the sound of enthusiastic applause and I was suddenly aware that the whole enterprise had been watched by the occupants of a car which had parked just above our gate. They had binoculars trained on us – quite a feat since we were only half a dozen yards away – and were obviously enjoying us extremely as a sort of additional perk of their chosen picnic spot. As we let ourselves out onto the road we could see two female shapes hunched over the open boot and the voice of one of them rang out with a weird echo as though her head were in a dustbin – 'Edie, would you like a little almond tart?'

One of the two men lowered his binoculars and raised a can of lager in jovial salutation, and we exchanged pleasantries. I explained that we were waiting for a possible lift into Osmotherley and the ladies clucked sympathetically.

Now hitch-hiking with three children is difficult unless you accept that you need thumb only Land-Rovers, vans, cattle wagons and charabancs. The average touring family don't have that much space available. I fixed my eyes on a spot in the middle distance where the road from Hawnby appears over Redway Head.

The binocular men had their instruments firmly trained on the same spot, obviously thoroughly immersed in our problem. Almond Tart looked truly concerned.

Car after car went by in the wrong direction, but when

one finally materialised which seemed to be going the right way, the picnickers hailed it enthusiastically on our behalf. 'Now you'll be all right,' they said.

'No,' I hissed at them. 'There isn't enough room,' I said desperately, 'and you don't take scruffy kids in a car like that.' It was an immaculate Daimler. But Almond Tart was undaunted. Sometimes, she asserted, such people are nicer than others. I took this to mean that, in her opinion, owning a Daimler doesn't necessarily make you a snob.

But, wonder of wonders, the Daimler was about to turn off the road and into our gate. I stepped forward, pointing out that I was the occupier of the place they were heading for, so I assumed I must be the object of their journey. They all got out and smiled.

Suddenly I was terrified. What could such people want? They had brief cases, one each, on the back seat. They looked legal. Debt collectors. Bailiffs. Social security sleuths. Secret police. One of them, obviously the leader, had a piratical black patch over one eye, and his charm was almost too much for a family of hippies.

He said that he and his two companions were from a Royal Commission on Historical Buildings and wanted to look over the house. It was such an unlikely tale that I knew at once they must be con men and I felt somehow better. After all, if they had come to case the joint, I could always help – if their experience of such things could show me that I possessed anything worth pinching, I'd help them load it into the car for a third-share!

Like the mother of the Gracchi, these tatty kids at my elbow were my only jewels. What had I to lose? I agreed, but pointed out that I must first get to the village for vital supplies. The piratical gentleman, almost too eager to be of assistance, turned the Daimler round, left one of the men to 'measure up' and loaded the children into the back. A tall young man sat beside them. He had a beard and eyes of a strange unearthly blue that I had only once seen before on one of the baddies in a Hitchcock film (*North by Northwest*, for the film buffs among you!)

Old Henry and the dog were back, peeping round the corner of the nearest building. Another neighbour had found something quite unnecessary to do where he could get a good view. Almond Tart and company beamed conspiratorially. A third neighbour drifted near, and they all watched as the driver, looking more like a Gestapo chief than ever, handed me politely into the front seat. As we drove off, I thought that the story would soon be round the dale that They had caught up with me at last and taken me off for questioning. I grinned.

I drew my Family Allowance, shopped and was brought back. The men came in and measured everything, and although I listened very carefully I didn't glean the slightest hint of hidden treasure. But they were very nice people – for crooks.

The following day I got a letter from the Estate office saying that I was shortly to be visited, at their invitation, by representatives of a Royal Commission on Historical Buildings, and they trusted that I would give them my full co-operation. And when I laid my ear to the grapevine, all I heard was that Her at Hagg House had gone off in a taxi.

But it was fun while it lasted.

'Mouseholes to hitch-hiking,' I said to my friends. 'I shall go into Osmotherley early with the chap who goes that way to exercise his dogs.'

I had been helping to pick potatoes and we were enjoying a cup of tea. The fire blazed merrily in the grate and it was raining coldly and persistently outside. I was vaguely aware that I was cutting it a bit fine, but I was enjoying my tea, the warmth, and the pleasure of good company. Later that night I was due at my adult education class in philosophy, but I didn't have many things to do before I went.

Even so, I did put a bit of a spurt on when my friends pointed out the time and suggested that I would have to hurry if I were going to catch the particular lift I had taken for granted in the bright warmth of their sitting room.

Highly Woolly, a pet lamb, and his friends were to be put in for the night. And I had to give him a dose of stomach medicine. And a helping of bramble leaves. I had had them inside for a day or two to help them accept hand feed and one another and let them out the day before, but Highly Woolly, the bouncy, thieving extrovert, was clearly not well and I was trying to counter his digestive disturbances with the means at my disposal. Of course, being in a hurry, I couldn't find him.

By the time I did, it was clear that I had missed my lift. I resigned myself to hitch-hiking in the rain.

Nothing looks more forlorn than a wet Swaledale lamb, and I was worried as I drove him gently back up the field, with his companions following behind. I pinned my faith on the armful of super-quality hay I had cadged for him – like grapes for an invalid – on the brambles I had gathered on the way back, and on the dark brown medicine in the bottle on the shelf.

I penned the lambs and went into the house, smiling to myself.

This strange brown concoction was probably as scientifically successful as James Herriot's Universal Cattle Medicine – in fact I was almost sure it was the same stuff – but it smelt invincible and I had a weird faith in it, having seen dramatic recoveries after it, even if not demonstrably because of it.

Having no light in the house, I put more money in the meter. This had no effect, and I realised we were in the grip of a power cut. Great.

I somehow measured 2 cc of the brew into a drench bottle and dosed the patient. In the process a lot of it went over my hand and into a cut on my finger, which I sucked thoughtfully. It tasted of molasses and coughdrops. I hunted fruitlessly in the dark for my textbooks, then changed and set off.

It felt a lot later than it was, because the clocks had gone back since I last made the journey and it was almost dark. I looked over my shoulder for a headlight approaching from the rear and saw nothing. The rain had slowed to a drizzle so I started to walk.

On my right, sheep and lambs rustled and squeaked as they foraged in a field of rape and turnips, but I could see only scuttling ghost-shapes in the gloaming. 'Dimpsy', they call it in Oxfordshire, this mysterious half-light. It's a comforting word, without menace in it, and I repeated it to myself as I walked to the next farm.

Through the window I could see George and Sandra eating their teas round an oil lamp. Then on down the steep hill, over the echoing beck and up again to another farm, where I could see lights moving outside.

This proved to be the delivery of the month's feedstuffs, accomplished by headlamp and flashlight. The assembled group laughed and chatted. Pity I wasn't going in the other direction, they said for I could have had a lift with the driver. The wind whistled round the corner and I agreed. But it wouldn't be long, I told myself, before someone came my way, and then I would reach Osmotherley in no time.

Up the hill, over the cattle grid and on to the moor. The road was now the same pale silver as the steamers of cloud but clear to see, even though the Beware of Sheep notice was unrecognisable, looking more like a rather butch witch, all square shoulders and pointed hat.

During the week I had walked this far with the children, in daylight, and we had talked of adding something to the notice – 'Drysies Rule – O.K.?' or a pair of antlers. We had been on our way to a jumble sale in the village hall and were full of happy anticipation. I remembered Robert, later that afternoon, four hats on his head, two ties flapping, a pair of penny spectacles on his nose, standing up on the platform posing with an incredible purple bra. On these rare and special days pocket money which won't stretch beyond a single chocolate bar, suddenly has limitless potential and ten pence can bring a skipping rope with ball-bearings and a real ball gown and still leave more than enough for a pair of red high-heeled shoes and a diamond brooch.

But this time I was on my way to a philosophy class in Northallerton and I was dressed accordingly. Already I was regretting the posh shoes and decent coat and wishing I were in wellies and donkey jacket. But I had worn wellies the night I went to enrol, and seeing them move across the parquet floor in the assembly hall at Allertonshire School is like a remembered nightmare. All those dreams of being suddenly naked on the Underground came true that day as the diamond-patterned soles impressed themselves on the polished wood and the assembled students.

Now this time it was the other way about and I felt ridiculous with my attempt at smartness slowly absorbing the relentless drizzle and my feet feeling gift-wrapped in those dreadful shoes.

How difficult it is to step from one role to another; but then I suppose people who try to cross the thresholds between different worlds must be prepared for the sort of jet-lag sensation that always complicates the transition.

Still no car came. I was on the long, straight section with the heather stretching away on either side. I suddenly remembered that I had not left any water with the lambs. I worried. I wondered how anyone could express an opinion on St Augustine's vision of the passage of time and be so stupid as to forget to water their livestock. I wondered how I could relate Taylor's Metaphysics to my last sight of Highly Woolly, staring into space with eyes that looked as though they had been breathed on.

Square Corner at last, and the yard light at Chequers Farm bright in the gathering dark. The lonely road suddenly populous, almost gay. Sheep feet busy on the metalled road ahead and at my left shoulder a gathering of young beasts behind a gate. As I broke into a run towards the blessed light ahead they did so too, and galloped merrily alongside in the dark, on the other side of the hedge.

If ever you come to this part of Yorkshire, someone will tell you that, in the days when Chequers was an inn, a turf fire burned in the hearth, year in, year out, and was never allowed to go out. It's a bit of local legend. When I was a little girl in London, they used to say something similar about the Windmill Theatre. Plus ça change, plus c'est la même chose.

Into Chequers for a packet of crisps and a telephone call to the friend waiting for me in Osmotherley.

Then the last stage of the journey, with a longlegged old ewe galloping ahead of me all the way to the last cattle grid.

* * *

The people at the moor gate were very quiet, staring straight at me until I caught their collective eye and then they all looked elsewhere in unnatural unison as though expecting me to believe that they had not been watching me. Then, one by one, their heads turned again and they continued their contemplation of what I was doing. I could feel their watchfulness like a cold draught on the back of my neck.

I couldn't really blame them. They had parked their car on the verge and got out – father, mother and three quite large children and come to the moor gate for a look at the view. Part of that view was a figure in wellingtons, with a sports bag over one shoulder and a polythene bread bag in the other, which it waved cheerfully at nothing in particular. Every now and then it gave a strange cry. There was no other living creature in sight. After a while a very small sheep crept out of the bilberries and stood watching, but as soon as the figure moved towards it, it scurried off to peer, as did the observers, from a place of safety.

The figure laid down the shoulder bag, made one or two adjustments to the contents, then rose and, ignoring the sheep, scattered something from the bread bag in a pile on the turf. Then it sat and waited. The sheep came and ate the offering. The human took no notice, just tipped another pile of goodies and retreated nearer to the other bag. Again and again this happened, until the two of them were only feet from the bag and inches from each other. Then the sheep was grabbed and apparently attacked, even wrestled to the ground – the watchers were agog.

When I finished clipping Sparrow I marked her, gave her a mouthful of worm paste and let her go. I wrapped the fleece and marched off the long way back through the brackens leaving my audience guessing. I grinned at the possible interpretations they could have brought to what they might have thought they had seen.

Later that night, a friend called for her son, who was playing with the twins, and told me that a group of travelling show people were busy setting up some kind of performance in the village and we all piled into the gallant little mini so as not to miss this phenomenon.

A man dressed in pink, dragging a dead dog, walked slowly to the centre of the village, followed by an elephant on stilts. He drove a circle of giant tent pegs around a bright red tree that had appeared on the green, feeling the three strange fruits that it bore, one of which looked disturbingly like a football bladder. His dog, now looking much better, was tied to one of the stakes. A house came slowly down the street from the other direction and parked beside the tree. From it came three yellow men with stiff beards and long hair. One carried a blunderbuss, one a linen-basket and the third a pair of sheep-shears, which amused me even more. I struggled in my head for a name to call them, a word to re-create them, and found 'Hittites' and clung to it because it fitted. They shot the pink man, clipped the fruits from the tree, and poured the lentils they contained into the linen basket. Then they produced a rocket on pram wheels from under a cloth and tied the pink man to it, wheeling him off up in the direction of the village hall.

I have not attempted to tell you the story – only what it was that I saw, because that is still the only thing I can be certain of. If my description sounds a little silly, ·I must hasten to say that it was not intended, in itself, to be a criticism, although my sense of humour was aroused by the scene. It was never intended to be described in words, which formed no part of the proceedings and the only way for you to see it clearly would be to see it with your own eyes rather than mine. I hope you get the chance – they call it the Journey of the Tree Man. But I did find it silly. At the time, though, I could not say why.

We were fortunate enough to meet the cast over supper, but I was a bit apprehensive before they arrived – after all, like the people who had watched me during the morning, I did not really know what it was I had been watching, and why should they have to be interested in what I might have thought I had seen? I made an effort to do more listening than talking and when I heard one of them saying that they were attempting to lift theatre away from the 'literary' I felt somehow got-at and said even less. I was interested to know whether the performance always felt the same to them and whether it would always look the same to me, but I didn't know how to establish either hypothesis. I felt at a loss, and it was clearly time I said something, so I thought perhaps I would complement the shining honesty of these young art students by asking something I genuinely wanted to know. I asked the man on my right what was the origin of the Tree Man's pink quilted suit. He said it was a dog-baiter's protective clothing and I laughed and told him I had called it, in my head, Samurai equipment. And suddenly a chink of light appeared and shone on the problematical performance, which was slowly turning itself upside-down.

Once when I was preparing some work for an art exam I was having great difficulty with some lettering. My art teacher told me to turn the work upside down, so that I would stop seeing the letters as I expected them to be and see instead simply the lines and curves I was dealing with. I have often found since that a less direct approach to many things is helpful. Perhaps I could see the Tree Man more clearly if I looked at it from a different direction.

I thought of the dog-baiter and the Samurai, and my Hittites, which to the person beside me, had been bearded ladies, and realised just how far the journey had, in fact, taken me. Right back to the roots of the red tree. The Coolabar Tree.

When I was very small, my mother used to sing Waltzing Matilda to me, and I asked her for it time and time again. I never told her the wonderful pictures that the words made for me, because I was too small to suppose that they were not correct, definitive. A Swagman was as strange in my head as the Tree Man in his protective clothing. The Sergeant was just a Sergeant, but the thoroughbred on which he rode was as weird as the stilty elephant and I suddenly found a second-hand word for the spirit of such beasts – Jabberwock. The troopers (one, two, three!) weren't yellow with hooped skirts, but they weren't the troopers my adult knowledge draws for me. I remember my father teaching me the poem that begins:-

> When I was but thirteen or so
> I went into a golden land,
> Chimborazo, Cotopaxi,
> Took me by the hand.

I could never understand why my classmates found it so obscure, yet found that when I tried to explain it for them, to make it come alive, I destroyed it just as surely as my description of the performance did. I find it so easy to grasp the concept of 'obscurity' in literature, the liberty granted to the imaginative vision by undefined language. Why had I found the reverse procedure so hard to accept? They showed me pictures and I made words, but they were as real and as valid as the picture of a billabong that frightened the life out of me as a toddler, in the days before I had listened to my art teacher's advice and before I had forgotten that the world is seen more clearly if you bend down and peer at it between your legs. I found the show silly because my words were silly –

Up came the Samurai
And fastened up his dangle-dog
Down came the Hittites, one, two, three.
They shot him, they got him,
　They dragged him off to Thimbleby
And pinched all the coolabars that grew on the tree.

I hope the I.O.U. Theatre won't be offended. I offer them this additional thought. If I had unlimited wealth, one of the things I would buy is Picasso's *The Three Musicians* because it has a sweet and special silliness that I find deeply moving.

It took an inordinate amount of thought to arrive at what must pass for a conclusion, and I lay in bed tired but at peace and ready to face great hosts of visual experiences. After all, I had proved to myself that I was not out of my depth. Merely out of my element. And being out of my element is something I experience at fairly regular intervals.

One of the big events in the life of most families is the christening of each new addition. A cakes and ale sort of affair, with not so many tears as a wedding and just as much jollity; a few hours' headwetting to precede a few years' bedwetting, if you like to look at it that way.

But I have no special way of looking at it. None of my children was christened at the usual age. Not being church-goers, it just didn't happen. They were named, numbered, registered, but never baptised. Since we do not attend a church, it has never been a matter of much concern.

Don't misunderstand me. I'm not an atheist. I've just

always found it rather difficult to express my beliefs through organised worship and have never found a label which fitted my own ideas. I have contented myself over the years with a commitment to a code of behaviour which I have tried to pass on to the children. You can look on it as independence or laziness according to your own views.

So it was a surprise, to say the least, when Andrew wrote a hurried letter from boarding school asking me to attend the church on Sunday because he was getting confirmed – and, as a necessary formality, baptised at the same time.

I had one of my usual panics. Of course I would go. But what must I do? Would he need godparents? My sister and brother-in-law, my brother – but they are all miles away. Would I have to name him? Did it matter where I sat in church? Should I wear a hat?

And this, of course, was the nub of the matter. Church confuses and frightens me because I'm not used to it. It's not simply a matter any more of leaving one's nets and coming to Him. You have to have the right gear, say and do the right things. I am fairly familiar with the original Book, but the script of the adaptation takes so many different forms that I feel spare in what always seem to be everybody else's churches.

That was how Andrew felt when he first went to this school. Church attendance is compulsory. He, though, in the grip of the same feelings of confusion and worry, did not dare go, and was hiding in town. He told me about this, and about his overwhelming dread that he would be caught. I told him I knew a way to avoid being found out and he brightened visibly. 'Tell the Headmaster,' I suggested. 'Lay it on the line. I'll write a note to help. No one can shoot you if you've already surrendered.' The Headmaster was wonderful, treating the matter just as I had hoped. And that's how Andy came to be taking confirmation classes. It was to help him understand the workings, the routine ins and outs, of the church he was to attend.

I wasn't prepared for a Road to Damascus. I didn't think my child would feel called. Of course I would go to the ceremony, but what, why, how? I worried myself through till the Sunday.

In church I felt as I had expected. It was big and modern and there were candles and a bishop in red robes but the people were all dressed with an informality that I found surprising. Jeans and beards. And I felt that neither aspect of it fitted what I looked for in a church. The ceremony began, and it was all read out of books and a great gathering of young people were confirmed at once, making it repetitive and somehow meaningless and most of the girls giggled. The ceremony was followed by Holy Communion. I had never attended such a service before and was fascinated, but somehow unmoved. I tried to join in the Lord's Prayer, but they were using some simplified version and I was embarrassed into silence.

The thought struck me that, following the written service so closely must make it almost impossible to give those words meaning time after time. I recalled the funerals I have attended in the village church, and my determination that I will, at my own end, do without the muttered jargon and settle for something off-the-cuff. As the people went in droves to the Communion rail, I realised with a hollow sense of loss what it was that was missing. He was not there.

I expect that, for each person making their own act of faith, He must have been apparent. Surely they wouldn't have participated in this rather silly-looking ceremony unless that were so. But I was fidgety and unsatisfied, just the mother of one of the queue of youngsters whose names were read off a card. Only the smile of the man who had been giving the confirmation classes seemed real. He had shown me where to sit and answered my most urgent questions kindly. But the surplice and the long scarf – a God-supporters scarf? – seemed to move him back out of reach. I longed for the service to finish. For me, He was not there.

After the ceremony was over, and Andrew was the possessor of a copy of the New English Bible, I was asked to stay for coffee. In the room behind the altar, cups rattled. I saw a woman step up to my son and put an arm round him. There was so much love in the gesture that I was taken completely by surprise. Seeing me she stopped, then smiled. She was so glad I could come. She and her husband had arranged to take Andrew out for lunch if I couldn't make it, so that he wouldn't feel left out. She was the wife of the man who had been so helpful when I arrived. The man who had taken the confirmation classes. And suddenly I realised the reason for the lad's apparent conversion. He had responded to these people. To their kindness, understanding and love. It had been something real after all.

I smiled my gratitude at the kind woman and we left for a day in town. It was a great relief to me to know that He whom I had hoped to find had been there after all. Even if we didn't meet up until the coffee.

'Faint Heart Never Kissed a Pig'

I had been writing my newspaper column for nearly four years when an article in the *Guardian* mentioned my name, presenting me to the great world as a provincial journalist worthy of a wider audience. There was a flutter of interest from one or two publishers which both flattered and frightened me. It was both what I wanted and what I dreaded.

Every writer has some goal, from selling a million and making a fortune to changing the world's thinking and making an impression. I suppose I see myself as a performer without the courage to stand up and perform. Each newspaper article, then, was a script which, in spirit, I delivered to an audience which had gathered over a period of time, so that they had become friends whom I met by appointment. I was preaching, if you like, to the converted. Now it had been suggested that I write a book, and older, forgotten dreams surfaced. Dare I re-enter the world I thought I had left behind? Having strived for so many years to be considered a competent, caring countrywoman, could I now confess to myself that I longed as deeply as ever to be recognised for qualities I was not even sure I possessed – literacy and wit.

The *Guardian*'s correspondent suggested that some publisher should seek me out in my rural fastness and several did. A prestigious publishing house asked for a sample chapter; an eager unknown sent a telegram offering immediate cash. I was out of my depth.

In my youth I had written many short stories. I thought they were good. I was Maupassant. I was Sansom. I was brought down to earth by each rejection, buoyed up to heady heights when they went into print. I got myself on the books of a literary agency and it was to them I turned in my time of trouble. To them I referred all approaches. In their hands the bubble burst and the surge of interest subsided.

With the perversity of reaction of a true Celt, I slipped into a profound depression. When the idea of the book was first mooted, I panicked. Just before I came to the dale, there lived here an elderly man whose fund of obscure sayings have delighted me as, one by one, I stumbled across them. 'As Old Arthur used to say' preceded many words of wisdom in the guise of apparent nonsense. One of my favourites is 'If things don't alter they'll stop as they are.' At first I laughed at this, along with everyone else, as one of the ramblings of a dear but silly old man stating the patently obvious. But when there seemed a likelihood of a flutter of fame, it threatened to jeopardise the very rural fastness in which I had somehow found a little solace, a grey furry peace into which I cowered like a self-satisfied matron in a woolly cardy. And suddenly Old Arthur's words of wisdom looked like the answer to the dilemma – if things don't alter, and only then, will they stop as they are. I didn't want to write a book, Did I?

But when the burst of interest in me and my way of life subsided and left me looking at it alone, like a child with a handful of pebbles, I fell victim to a black misery that urged me to send them as far from me as my disappointed rage could fling them. They were not jewels at all. I had grown up.

The people whose affection and respect I sought were jealous and resentful. The creatures whose welfare I worked for were a self-indulgent luxury and the love they seemed to give me in return for the loyalty my fellow-humans regarded so lightly was no more than ill-disguised greed. I wanted a little recognition, a little acclaim. I wanted to write a book.

And into that celtic twilight came Harry.

Harry was the northern area representative of the publishers with whom I eventually signed. He sent me a letter in his gloriously haphazard handwriting by way of introduction, inviting me out to lunch. And suddenly I had something else to think about which, in itself, did me a power of good. The simple fact of being invited out to lunch by a man, even by way of business, was so much of a novelty to one now accustomed to business that concerned nothing more potentially testing than catching sheep, lifting bales or coming to terms with an illiterate typewriter that the whole thing filled me with a dreadful foreboding.

They say that social graces dinned into small children last a lifetime and can be called into service whenever necessary, but of the hundred-and-one theoretical situations in which I imagined myself as I re-read the letter yet again, I could not see myself coping. After all, it's not a hundred years ago that I sat in the farmhouse next door, my mouth stuffed like a marmoset's with prune-stones as I scanned anxiously from face to face across the table to ascertain, if I could, what the rest of the guests were doing with theirs. To be frank, I never did catch them doing anything positive; I eventually swallowed mine.

Social naivete can be attractive in a young girl stepping for the first time into society, but in a middle-aged woman it is rather nauseating. I told myself that if I relaxed it would all come back to me like riding a bicycle, and pushed to the back of my mind the memory of what happened when I got the old velocipede out for the first time after the snow. That was not a pretty sight.

I told three people about the invitation and all of them said exactly the same thing – what was I going to wear? Dammit, how did I know? I thought they had envisaged my going in jeans and wellies and felt slightly offended, but at the same time had to allow that they had, as the French say, reason. I don't often wear anything else.

A skirt seemed essential. I resurrected one from the back of the wardrobe and buried it again hastily. The relative inactivity of winter had added an inch or two round the middle and it was clearly necessary to look for something a little more generous. And tights. There were none without holes so the problem of footwear was solved. It had to be knee-boots, which, with the rather over-long skirt I had plumped for, as you might say, left no ladder visible.

At this stage I looked out the contents of the make-up wallet my sister-in-law gave me. I had a go, using the electric light in the bedroom. Then I went to spy out of the sitting-room window to see what the pony was up to and caught sight of what appeared to be an elderly oriental, peering out alongside. It was only when its jaw sagged simultaneously with mine and its lips silently framed the same expression of extreme stupefaction that I realised it was my own daylight reflection in the mirror.

This was the expensive all-in-one make-up I had bought for my sister's wedding, so carefully matched to my complexion by the little dollfaced lady in the quiet-carpeted store.

I filled my cupped hands with baby lotion and melted off most of the awful yellow mask. I remember the saleslady asking me where I had got the tan she had evidently matched up to the contents of the tube and recalled the momentary lowering of monumental eyelashes when I told her 'Yorkshire'. Perhaps she had done it on purpose. I refuse to believe I have ever been that colour, even at the height of summer.

Then Harry himself knocked at the door. I pulled on the first thing the hand of modesty could lay hold of in the open drawer, and was halfway to the door before I discovered that it was my son's green sailing jacket.

My host, I discovered, had decided on knee-breeches, with leather sandals and a black Labrador called Sam by way of accessories.

I, half-crazed with relief, kept the sailing jacket on and thoroughly enjoyed myself, rediscovering all the pleasure – not exactly sensual, but pleasure none the less – of spending time with a man to whom charm came naturally and who went out of his way to make me feel like a woman of some importance. He asked what I most enjoyed eating, and when I confessed that, for the previous few years, fish and chips had been a sought-after treat, he 'refused to waste tournedos Rossini' on me, and we ate duck with orange sauce. His occasional loving references to a wife he clearly valued were a relief and a comfort. We saved the chocolate mints that came with the coffee for Sam, and at the end of the day he accepted the guinea-fowl eggs that were everyday fare for us as though they were the rarest truffles. I met him just once more.

Before the book was finished, Harry was found dead in his car and I felt I had lost a friend.

And so *Faint Heart Never Kissed a Pig* came to be written. For Harry and for Sam. For the creatures who had become part of our lives, for the people among whom I was living, by way of the explanation they so clearly needed. For the friends I made through my newspaper columns, for the children and for myself. And for money.

I needed to write a book to bring it all together, this dreaming and striving, this childish insistence on a simplistic approach to livestock husbandry which so many people dismissed as anthropomorphism but which was proving time and time again to be not only valid practice but sound economic sense. I had things I wanted to say, axes I needed to grind. There were points that I felt I could now ponder in public and I was ready to be judged. I set to work.

And alongside the preparation of the book, life went on in

the special way of the countryside – not in a circle, endlessly repeating itself, but in a spiral, taking the repetitive, curving course through the same four seasons with their tasks and problems, yet never covering the same ground twice. And writing the book was hard, because I was telling of what had happened then while it was happening now, and knowing that it would all happen again, and I was trying to write about ignorance from a position of knowledge which I was still trying to increase. I was living on a succession of different levels and each day was like running up and down stairs. But I finished it.

One of the things that had to happen before the pile of dog-eared papers could become a hard, square book was for someone to design a cover. But that was not my responsibility so I waited to see what would happen. On the second Friday in July I was asked once again to help at a further-off farm on their annual clipping day. All day I caught sheep, hundred after hundred of them, and most of the time I was alone in the pen with them, grabbing, turning, dragging and then dosing and passing one sheep after another all through a long, hot day. And it was heaven.

Halfway through the day, though, I had a visitor. A photographer had come from London to take pictures for the book, and he was clearly alarmed by the noise, heat, smell and violence which is seen to be controlled only by those who know what's going on.

He agreed to return at night.

I limped home, bruised and battered, and was greeted by an eager photographer and a friend who had come, complete with children, to collect a little black goat called Doris and a pretty painted cart which she was to pull in the following day's Osmotherley Summer Games, giving rides to toddlers. My friend, in her fresh summer clothes, had taken charge of the situation. I heard the photographer ask if old Gertie the goat was pregnant. 'No', said my friend, brightly, 'Just grossly overfed,' and I felt really angry. How dared she suggest I had so little understanding of my creatures as to 'grossly overfeed'.

Afterwards I realised that this particular, and good, friend always used the word 'grossly' where anyone else would use 'very'. The criticism inferred was not implied. And anyway the photographer wouldn't be making that sort of judgment.

Lord, I was tired. I felt filthy and miserable, but dared not apologise.

The light was going fast, I know, but all the same I could have combed my hair, washed my face, changed out of the green, slimy plimsolls or even put on a little discreet make-up. But I didn't dare.

Do you know, I was so painfully embarrassed that I couldn't bring myself to go indoors and do it. I had this sort of desperate feeling that if I pleaded a need for the lavatory I could slip into my room and do something to repair the day's damage, but I couldn't face the certainty of my friend's noticing and saying encouragingly 'that's better,' thereby drawing attention to my vanity.

I was so embarrassed that I opted for posterity's seeing me 'warts and all', but after he'd gone I couldn't help feeling that just a little smidgin of mascara would have been a good idea. It was like having made a mess of an 'O' level exam and only realising as the final bell rang. It was another encounter with the problem of presenting two images at once and again I failed to cope.

I have hated that cover photograph with all my heart ever since.

The book was due to be released the following spring. I got a letter in the autumn from the publishers, asking if I would be willing to participate in any publicity appearances they might be able to arrange, so that I might promote the book. This came as a surprise, and my response to it, too, was something I found equally surprising. I wanted to appear on TV. I wanted to be interviewed. I wanted to prove to all the people who had hitherto only read me on a flat printed page, that I had dimensions they never suspected. I wanted to show them that I really did live in the very place that I had described, that I was real. I wanted, too, to show Jim and George and all the rest that in some of my spheres of activity I was not an apprentice. I was not always second-best, paddling up like an eager puppy and participating in things second-hand. I had tried so hard to earn a place in this little community by working with the families nearby, taking part in all the seasonal jobs, telling myself it was all part of my attempt at self-sufficiency, but I knew in my heart that it was nothing of the kind.

What I was really doing was begging from these, my immediate neighbours. Begging for their acceptance, their help, their friendship, their love. And if they were too blind to see it, how could I blame them? For ten years I had successfully deluded myself on the subject.

When I set out on my smallholding project, I had been utterly determined that I should not fall into the trap of presenting myself as a lone female, fallen upon hard times, asking the menfolk for their assistance. That way, I felt sure, would lead to jealousy and friction from the wives and womenfolk.

No, I would be a free spirit, floating in an aura of sexlessness, earning the assistance I needed from my fellow-farmers by trading the jobs I could do for the skills I had yet to learn. What a fool I had been. By doing just this, I had thrown down the gauntlet to the very wives and womenfolk I sought to reassure. Now I was meeting their menfolk not as another woman, calling their femininity in question – a challenge they could have met, but as a colleague, an equal, a fellow headman of another tiny tribe. In fact, the one role a wife in these parts could never fulfil. I had lost before I even began, and had taken ten years to find that out.

And so I would appear on TV and become, for a little while, a celebrity, a nine-days'-wonder. I would be offhand

and throwaway. I would cultivate a matter-of-fact approach to my sudden importance.

And then Sid came, late at night, to tell me that Jim had made a fairly successful attempt to amputate his right hand on his sawbench, and all the adolescent arrogance and self-pity swirled away like tealeaves down a plughole and I felt empty and sick. So I had written a book. So what?

I went back with Sid to offer what comfort I could to Flora, and to plan with her how we could run the farm till Jim came out of hospital. I have never worked harder.

*   *   *

It was all over bar the shouting, and there was plenty of that as Jim took the reins once more into his mended hand and Flora resumed hostilities, when I returned home one night to see Sam the labrador, walking down the hill, followed by Harry's stepson Adrian, who had taken over Harry's job with the publishers. They had come to tell me that the wheels had begun turning, the machinery had been set in motion to launch my book. It was happening at last, and the days out with Adrian, at signing sessions and radio interviews, and the days at home, entertaining film crews and trying to talk wittily while ensuring that goats did not chew vital wires, that pigs did not sink fangs into technicians' legs and sheep did not shit on camera, all mingled oddly with the spring tasks that overtook the smallholding and the few jobs I still did for Jim. It happened so very fast, like an audition for which I was not fully prepared, like a chance that I was somehow missing, even while I held it in my hand.

However you look at it, from up or from down, the Monday of the week my book was published was a pretty eventful day.

It began early, because one or two of Jim's cows, whose daily care I still shared, were very near calving and I wanted to make sure they were all right.

I was especially looking forward to seeing the big, black Galloway whose baby, I felt sure, would be with us now. The night before she had withdrawn from the others, watching wistfully as I put a gate on the entrance to her favourite field. 'Sorry,' I told her, 'but I'm making sure you can't get down to the river. No drowned calves or freezing rescues. I'm getting too old for that sort of thing.'

In the grey early light I ran down to the place I'd seen her choose, but she wasn't there.

So then began the systematic search that the owners and guardians of beef suckler herds will know well, all around the hedgebacks and copses; under all the walls. I came across a little dun Galloway with calving on her mind, but she hadn't actually settled to the job so I left her and searched for the black one.

In the end, after three-quarters of an hour, I found her back in the shed, looking hopeless, a dark red discharge soiling her hindquarters. She rose stiffly when I went in and stood looking at me, an appeal in her lovely eyes.

'What's wrong?' I asked her, but I didn't expect any answer. I'd have to fetch Jim. What could I say when he came to the door? That all was not well? How could I, with my lack of experience, be sure of that? But sure I was, deep down, and I shouted up to Nancy to get her own breakfast while I ran to get help.

At the door I hesitated again. Then took a deep breath, knocked, and said simply that I was worried. Jim came, looked, then sent for the vet, vindicating my judgment, but I felt dreadful all the same. One or two remarks from Flora seemed to suggest that my presence might have precipitated trouble, if trouble there was, and I worried until the vet's car came. After all, I might have made it happen, just by being there, by being me. I might have made whatever it was come about without even being conscious of it. And I prayed hard that the worst, which I feared, might not happen. That the dead calf I suspected might by some miracle turn out to be alive. That I might play the heroine just this last once before being assigned forever the role of villainess.

But when the vet left there lay in the golden straw two fine calves, both alive, both tottering soon on shaky legs to find the teats of the dear black cow who crooned with delight at her double blessing.

I was so beside myself with joy and pride that all the fear went spinning away on a great tide of relief and when the little dun Galloway calved at lunchtime it was an anti-climax by comparison.

And in the evening, when Nancy came home from school, we went together along the bridleway to see if other neighbours had any fifty pence pieces for our meter. The house waited, cold and dark, for our return.

I saw something white at the edge of the wood and went closer to see. It was a fine white cat caught in a snare and I scrabbled in vain at the wire which was round her body just above the hips, squeezing her into a deformed wasp-waisted thing with hind legs swollen and stiff.

I used some dreadful language. It seemed to help as I hacked futilely at the wire which mocked the pocket-knife I carried. The cat belonged, poor creature, to a house ahead and I sent Nancy to fetch the owner and some wirecutters while I tried again to free her.

It was Smudge. I knew her well. Her front paws scrabbled feebly as I lifted her, snare and all, back over the branch she had leaped in her agony, and I loosed the snare from its retaining end and freed her as gently as I could. Her cries are with me still. I set off to her home. Her owner met me and carried his injured pet. His wife wept.

And despite everything poor Smudge died. All I had achieved was to allow her to go at home before the fire instead of alone in the wild, wet wood. That wasn't enough.

Yes, it was an eventful day, looked at from up. And from down. I tried hard to shelve my bucolic preoccupations and concentrate on my public image.

But on the eve of publication day a new complication arose.

I can't say that it was on the stroke of midnight, because I was out in the pigsty and couldn't hear the clock, but it must have been thereabouts.

Rosalie had started farrowing in the late afternoon and after an hour or so of preparatory grunting and shuffling that sounded from outside like a confrontation between sumo wrestlers the first pig announced its arrival with a disgruntled squeal.

By the time I had finished opening the steel outer door that was specially-made to contain our dear, but now vast sow, and crept gently to peep, two little ones were at the teat and as I watched a third was born, sneezed, stood up, and scuttled beneath Rosalie's uplifted hind leg to find out what it was that had so captivated her siblings.

And this little pig was, without doubt, the smallest pig I had ever seen!

At this point it was apparent that all was progressing perfectly normally, and so I went off to find someone to talk to to keep me from making a nuisance of myself and getting in Rosalie's way.

When I returned Rosalie was grunting happily with twelve fine piglets, one for each teat and the little one pushed to the back and squeezed underneath, but sucking as though milk were about to be declared illegal.

The afterbirth had begun to appear and I waited for it. Then, all of a sudden, a thirteenth pig arrived and what had been a harmonious supper party turned into an unseemly brawl.

There was no room for number 13. She had had nothing. She could get nothing. She was a fine, large pig, but dopey, weak and not aggressive enough to fight for a teat.

I felt grieved. The last thing I wanted was a pet pig. Messy, demanding, depriving me of the precious beauty sleep that I needed badly if I were to impress the TV cameras that were coming to see me next day.

I just didn't want to be bothered with a little pig. And as the thought came, so it went. I realised that I had taken the first step into the trap I had sworn to avoid.

With the excitement of the book, the fun of the publicity, I had taken a step away from the very principles on which it had all been founded.

And I reached out and chose my pig.

Not the thirteenth pig herself – her need for Rosalie's milk was paramount, but the third pig, the tiniest-ever, the pinkest, the most beautiful. Replete and content she lay in my hand, her ears still folded for storage and her tiny trotters white and perfect against my grubby palm. She was unaware that her life, so soon begun, was to take a strange new turn.

And an hour later I made up her first bottle. I still didn't know what to call her, but I referred to her as 'her indoors', to distinguish her from 'them outside'. And when the first film crew arrived, she stole the show.

I spent the following Friday afternoon sitting in a branch of W.H. Smith in Bradford, waiting to sign copies of the book for anyone who might call and buy one. And nobody did.

Well, it wasn't exactly a surprise – Bradford is untrodden ground as far as I am concerned and I don't expect anyone had heard of me there. One short and rather pleasant interview on local radio half-an-hour before the signing session wasn't enough to burn me on the public consciousness like pokerwork on a wooden tray, so to speak. But all the same I didn't feel much like a best-selling author, as you can imagine.

And four days later, in the very small hours of the following Tuesday morning, I was kneeling beside my beloved Snuff, who had given so many Press and TV interviews herself just lately and was fast becoming one of the best-known sheep outside the carpet advertisements. Like some terrible nightmare the scene of her very first lambing was playing itself out all over again and I beheld once more the swollen, grinning head of a lamb that had been trapped fast by an accidental misplacement of his forelegs within the ewe, but this time, for the first few awful moments of discovery, I believed that Snuff herself had died in the attempt to deliver it. She was flat on her back, her legs stiffly extended and her poor swollen body deathly still.

But she was breathing, and I laid her more comfortably and removed the huge floppy lamb, half steaming hot, half icy cold, flinging it angrily onto the straw in the carefully-prepared lambing-pen while I addressed myself to the comfort and safety of old Snuff, dearest and best of friends.

Another, smaller lamb waddled out from a dark corner and wailed. Snuff muttered and tried to rise. I gave her this lamb to occupy her, just as doctors had once given me a fine, healthy twin, while they tried to hide the other from me till they were sure he would breathe, move, live.

But the huge lamb still lay immobile. It breathed loud, rattling gasps, drawn into lungs that were squeezed beneath flattened ribs. Its shoulders looked grotesque, apparently dislocated, and the great head with the closed puffy eyes, like a rabbit with myxomatosis, was clearly too heavy to lift. I despaired of it.

And even as I did so, I noticed that the other lamb had fallen weakly to the ground, and I could see that he had what appeared to be a hernia where the umbilical cord left his belly and Snuff, clearly distressed by this, was biting and chewing at it. As a result the poor little chap was bleeding in a swift and steady stream.

I grabbed him and ran indoors, tied off the small remaining tag of cord with sewing cotton, sprayed the whole mess with antibiotic and sped to phone the vet.

He could offer no magic formula, no promise of success, and I finally handed back to Snuff a puny son, too weak to stand, wearing a truss made of crepe bandage and over this a sort of romper suit constructed from a pair of tights, with the gusset removed to let his little bottom stick out, and the waistband stitched up round his neck. I held out no hope for the big lamb. By lunchtime he had not managed to stand. Snuff was plainly worried.

I milked out a cupful of golden colostrum and fed it to these poor broken babies. Hourly I tended them, often crying with the sheer weariness and the realisation that I wasn't exactly qualifying for Shepherd of the Year, either.

Almost all the people who came to interview me asked how I cope alone and at that moment I realised that most of the time I don't. Things just happen around me and I catch up now and then. That was what I told the YTV programme researcher who called in the midst of this to ask if I would agree to their TV vet doing a spring-on-the-farm programme from my poor stricken smallholding the following Thursday. I stared at her with red rimmed eyes and nodded weakly. She seemed to think that the little lamb and his homespun surgical appliance would be a good thing to show the viewers and drove off really happy. I went back into the house, utterly shattered, to find that the cats had eaten two pounds of cheese.

But at last when I went to the barn the big lamb had managed to get to his feet and the little one had found a teat all by himself and was wagging his wobbly tail while Snuff licked the bits that protruded from his silly suit. And I went, at last, to bed.

The day we were visited by the TV vet was an extremely jolly one. It began well, because the beautiful young woman who was to conduct the interview turned out to be easy going, helpful, and very good company. She cheerfully loaded her car with bags of animal feed that I would otherwise have had to carry down on my shoulders before the programme could be recorded. I had learned from recent experience that it is possible to promise a cameraman almost any shots he cares to suggest, provided you can choreograph the movements of the four-legged subjects by judicious placing of heaps of food, and almost all of them can be persuaded to beam for the viewers provided one plies them with a constant stream of dairy nuts from behind the camera. It was my observation during this brief period of public exposure that whenever a film crew had been at the house, I ended the day with a headache and the livestock with diarrhoea.

When the vet himself arrived, he was at some pains to point out that he was somewhat out of his element in the farm environment, having concentrated his skills more on the urban small-animal side of the practice. I saw what he meant. It wasn't so much that he was unused to the animals, it was more that he betrayed a townsman's optimism in his immaculate dress. A beautiful silver-grey sports jacket that seemed destined, I thought gloomily, to be pissed upon by at least one of the babies he was to show to the viewers. Snuff's lambs were toddling behind her now, and didn't take kindly to being picked up and cuddled. It scared them, and scared animals usually react in this one totally predictable manner. As a concession to the rural scene, he wore wellingtons, but for some reason they irritated me profoundly. They were too new, too spotless, and shone daffodil-yellow over the corrugations of what had for weeks been a sea of slimy mud and was only now beginning to scab over in the sunshine of spring's first few fine days. I wished that his boots were as muddy as mine.

The interview wasn't too harrowing. Throughout it I clung to Snuff's little son, still in his special suit, while Snuff stood beside me to make sure I didn't harm him. I explained in fumbling detail how he came to be so attired, and showed how I had left his hindquarters free because ewes like to sniff the backsides of their young ones as they suckle, just to make sure they've got the right lamb. Then I put him down, and up he ran to Snuff, who demonstrated right on cue just what I'd been saying. 'Well, look at that!' cried the TV vet. 'We must get another shot of that . . .' and Snuff and I looked at one another. We were getting to be old hands at this filming game. I gathered up both lambs, and the vet and I ran off with them a short distance, loosed them like greyhounds, and the cameras whirred again as the two little bodies shot in below Snuff's belly, sucking and sucking and twirling their tails while the old lady sniffed first one then the other and everyone applauded her as though she had done an impression of Anna Karenina on the railway platform. She turned her back on them all and walked away, her babies bobbing behind her as they all three sauntered out of shot.

The vet held, chatted to and talked about most of the animals. The little pig, who was now quite a TV veteran and was called Amelia, supped her bottle for the delighted camera crew, and the cats licked up the drips that fell from her slavering jaws. And suddenly I saw all these things, which had been throughout all these last worrying days a wearying succession of furred and feathered liabilities, through the eyes of these urban visitors, these highflying media-persons whose world I was beginning to envy. And I saw them for the treasures they really are. I had written about them and demonstrated their foibles so many, many times, that I had almost lost sight of their magic, regarding it only as something I myself had created. Not so, I realised, as the assembly Goshed and Goodlorded, restoring to me my own wonder at the specialness of my collected companions.

'Let's have a shot of John with the pony,' said the director. 'We've got a bit of footage left' and two technicians were despatched to catch Magnus who was two fields away where I had hidden him among Jim's cows. Now I felt in my water that this was not at all a good idea, as Magnus was exceptionally fit and likely, as a result, to be exceptionally silly. He had not long been turned loose and would not take kindly to being fetched home again so soon. But I said nothing and after the technicians had admitted themselves defeated by his Thelwellian technique of sitting down in response to their cajoling, I went to fetch him myself.

I led him into the yard, slipped off the lead-rein and went to get a carrot or two to give to the vet so that he could get the dratted pony's attention for as long as it took to pose the pair to the director's liking. But, like a fool, I forgot to shut the yard gate and when he saw that I had gone and left him in this place that was no longer his familiar yard but rather a tangle of weird wires and alien implements, not to mention a row of eager faces, he kicked up his heels and ran back into the field, peeping round the corner of Jim's cowshed. Between him and the vet was a piece of ground that looked much the same as the grubby yard, but I knew different. The crisp grey crust concealed a kneedeep accumulation of soft, silky mud squeezed between the toes of twenty-odd cows twice a day on their way to and from their hay ration. I looked again at those spotless yellow wellies and suggested that since the mountain looked like staying precisely where it was, perhaps Mahomet should make the first move.

Carrot in hand, the vet stepped confidently towards the pony, who peered round the corner at him with obvious interest. The carrot had clearly got his attention. Gradually, the yellow wellies sank into the mire, one step at a time until only their drawstring tops were visible, but Magnus' velvet nose was almost within reach. The vet extended the carrot at arm's length but Magnus, deciding it smelled more like a rat, kicked up his heels once again and sped off to rejoin the cows where he had left them. Following his madcap progress, spinning in a graceful arc above his retreating hindquarters and falling ineffectually into his slipstream, came a carrot.

*　　*　　*

At half past six on a sharp, frosty morning, with the grey early light only just showing up the sheep from the goats and the stars still gleaming yellow in the pallid sky a strange figure strode along the moor road.

At the lower end a pair of oversized boots plopped and echoed around a pair of frozen feet and at the other a strange impassive face glared at the wakening world. A face that was hardened into a fixed grimace of a ghostly grey-green. Not, as you may by now be supposing, the incredible hulk his hideous self, but yours truly getting ready for a trip to Leeds, and trying to do two or three things at once.

I don't often have days out in what I have come, from my present standpoint, to regard as civilisation, and I felt like making a bit of a special effort, so at sixish, there I was rummaging about in the dressing-table drawer once again among the collection of antique aids-to-nature that I seldom see a need to employ.

There I found a little tube of cucumber freshening mask, and as I hadn't had occasion to freshen any cucumbers for quite some considerable time, I was intrigued. It was, I read, a face pack that would smooth and refine the ageing epidermis and in these early hours the first fingers of daylight pointed accusingly at a multitude of little oversights that could do with erasing.

So I spread on a generous dollop of the grey-green goo and then looked to see what came next in the regenerative process. My heart sank as I read that the stuff should be left in-situ for ten to twenty minutes.

I didn't have that much time to spare – not if I wanted to be up the hill in time to feed the sheep before the taxi came. So I thought I'd feed the sheep first, while the cement was setting, then come down and wash it all off again. It seemed like a good idea.

And that's how the shuffling sasquatch came to be making its painful way, a bale on its back and a bucket in its hand, along the moor road in the small hours of a Monday morning.

By the time I reached the sheep, the stuff on my face had set solid, and I muttered my greeting through lips that were being drawn into a ghastly grin by the solidifying surface that was shrinking as it dried like the skin on a rice pudding. My nose was running in the keen frosty air and it itched urgently. I ran all the way home.

As I passed the kitchen window I looked in and my reflection gawped back, eyes peeping from the ashen face like cigarette burns in a tablecloth. I went in and washed it off.

Whether I looked any different I couldn't really decide, but no one, I told myself decisively, could say that I hadn't tried. I went upstairs to soak myself in a hot bath.

I was getting ready to go to a TV studio in Leeds for an afternoon chat show. The water felt all thick and funny because I'd had a houseful of children at the weekend who'd just managed to break all the glasses and the only one left was a Christmas present, two-thirds full of bathsalts which looked and smelt more like the washing soda they really were than the gardenia they purported to be.

So, in order to have a glass for my orange juice, I tipped the whole lot into my tub and felt like Cleopatra for ten lovely minutes before I was brought back to reality by the unmistakable sound of a hungry piglet whose stomach firmly believed its throat was cut.

When I got out of the taxi to open the gate onto the road I picked my path carefully. The viewing public would be expecting something rural to drop from my lips – I was more concerned lest it should drop from my shoe.

And the funny thing is, when I got to the studio, it seemed as if it was the most natural thing in the world for me to be there and I talked about my tumbledown, scruffy home to the cheerful, pleasant interviewer, but it seemed so far away, a whole different world. And so it is.

The publicity was fun, but it was like taking a lift from one level of reality to another. I tried always to tell the truth to my new urban friends; I hoped to keep faith with my rural ones. The woman being powdered for the TV cameras was the same one who totes bale and bucket, and the woman who showed off her sheep so proudly really does worm them, clip them, lamb them when necessary and tend them in all weathers. I am real. Aren't I?

But just when I really begin to doubt, to question that, there comes a sweet sunny day like the one that followed this last TV appearance and all the hurts and worries shrivel up and go crisp and flat like frogs on a motorway.

One, two – three at the most days before we were an island in a sea of soul-destroying slurry, and you couldn't get to the barn without wellies and now I could negotiate the round trip in carpet slippers.

Now the little pig, hiccuping occasionally, lay asleep at my feet in a pool of sunshine strained through the small panes of the window. Glory be to God for dappled things . . .

Amelia the pet pig (author's photo)

Silk Purses

For some businesses, the first actual earnest of success may be the first export order, for some the first million pounds' profit. On a smaller scale, perhaps the expansion of the workforce to double figures or the satisfactory completion of the first, vital contract. But for me there was no question – I knew I had made it the day the Ministry of Agriculture allocated me a holding number and agreed an official stocking limit and a financial limit in relation to hill livestock compensatory allowance claims. It was laughably small compared to my neighbours' holdings but it was real. The sheep could now receive their annual government subsidy and there was nothing Sandra could do about it. I was a hill farmer, and I had the papers to prove it.

It was time to move forward. As a spectacular culmination to the publicity connected with my first book, I had the honour to be invited to address a Yorkshire Post literary luncheon. The speech I gave didn't go down too badly, and after it was all over I sat in the foyer of a Bradford hotel, signing copies of my book alongside a peer of the realm, a media personality and a professor of English Literature, all of whom had recently published books. People who had bought copies of the books at the function came up to have them signed and a gratifying number were scrawled upon by my tenpenny ballpoint before the furore died down and only the famous TV presenter continued to sign book after book, with what looked suspiciously like a real gold pen. A lady came up to my table and introduced herself. She had written to me once or twice, and had bought a ticket to the luncheon just so that we might meet. We talked about animals for a while and she told me I was missing a lot by not having cattle on the farm. I told her I shared the day-to-day care of my neighbour's herd, but she said it was never quite the same as owning your own cow. When she left, she had given me three things, a jar of marmalade, some home-made cookies, and the beginnings of an idea.

We had a family conference over half term and decided to go ahead. We now have a cow and her name is Charity.

Not quite as simple as that, of course, and when I look into the pen at the back of the barn and see the heap of red-gold in the pale straw my stomach still does a somersault and I wonder just what I have taken on this time.

It was time, I felt sure, to take on something new. There would be some royalties to come from the book, and there was a sad gap to fill. Amelia, the TV pig, had been sold the day before the literary luncheon and although it was high time for her to go out into the world I missed her terribly.

And so Charity is here, a pedigree Jersey heifer. All legs and eyes, first in the home-made pen and then the wonder of outdoors, with daisies and butterflies and madcap gallops that end in total collapse in the dappled shadows under the plum trees.

Summer came suddenly, taking everything by surprise, as usual. And this summer was sweetened by the joy of starting something new. Our Cow.

And one day, God willing, that's what she'll be, this soft and silly innocent.

Meanwhile we take each day as it comes and Charity plays in a world where all creatures live in harmony and the most terrible thing they come across is the old rooster on his travels. Pedigrees are only bits of paper after all and every day is just to spend until it's all gone and the incredible eyelashes sweep down on the golden cheeks and rise again in wonder at the next, new morning.

And suddenly all I've ever learned about cows and their calves is all secondhand and hearsay and I, too, am beginning on something new.

'The friendly cow, all red and white, I love with all my heart.' I quoted as Charity lay across my legs in the sunshine. She sighed, as though she had heard it all before. The extraordinary humming-bird tongue flicked out; it's tip tentatively searching the recesses of one dewy nostril.

Charity is a very good name for the sort of cow I have in mind. Charity, as St Paul says 'is not easily provoked'. I slid my stiff legs carefully from under her sleeping form and went to milk the goats for her tea. As I passed her again with the brimming bucket I added aloud the most important attribute of all. 'Charity Suffereth long,' I advised her. 'And is kind.'

With the autumn came the annual making up of the moor flock.

One of the highlights of the year, for me, is the annual sheep sale organised by Northallerton Auctions for the farmers in this, the farflung hinterland of their catchment area. Down to the lowlands they come, load after load of hill sheep, their tousled coats and horned heads giving them a sort of wild, undomesticated appearance that is more than borne out by their behaviour as they leap over, smout under and weasel through barriers that their mighty daughters, the Mules and Mashams, have come to consider insurmountable. This year the sale was more of a success than ever as the farmers come slowly to accept that their County Town at last acknowledges their part in the pattern of sheep husbandry for which Yorkshire is justly famous. The sale has progressed by leaps and bounds from that first, tentative experiment, which ran concurrently with the weekly fatstock sale and was prevented only by the expenditure of much human sweat – some of it mine – from becoming a memorable cock-up in a tin hat.

But that's why I enjoy it so much. They said it wouldn't work. Farmers muttered that Northallerton was the wrong place for such an event. That there wasn't room for another hill sheep sale. And I felt a little surge of fellow-feeling for the organisers of the sale. After all, I've been swimming against the tide to some extent myself in trying to make single-handed success of this smallholding, and when I took the first few draft ewes from my small but precious flock to Northallerton rather than anywhere else, it was a gesture of solidarity, as it were, with fellow starters-from-scratch.

They, in their turn, have repaid me by invariably taking as much time and trouble over selling the lots I am able to put forward, which are, of necessity, only small, as over the large lots of quality stock they handle every market day. My gratitude for that courtesy is very great.

I didn't have much to sell at this year's annual sale. Just a few draft ewes. The idea is that, as they begin to get a bit older, the blackfaced ewes from the moors are sold to farmers with better grassland and crossed with the Teeswater and Leicester rams to breed the Masham and Mule ewes that rear a large proportion of the country's fat lambs, and my few had reached the time of life when it was advisable that they should join the draft down-country. I was sad to see them go, but hoped for a pleasant retirement for them, and a bit of profit for the men who bought them.

It was a bit of a milestone, really. I don't suppose the new owners of those ewes realised they were taking home a bit of history. In a way I hope they didn't. But those ewes were the last of the original sheep with which I began the flock and now up on the moor, waiting to begin all over again, I have only ewes with my own personal earmark. Ewes I have raised from lambs I have bred myself from those first, cherished originals. Sheep whose little eyes first blinked open on a world that contained, among other things, me. A towering figure with a loud voice, I became part of their lives and they of mine from their first April days. Not one on whom their first sun has set without having felt the touch of my hand. And I am as fiercely proud of them as any of the other farmers at the annual hill sheep sale.

To every rule there is an exception. To every sweeping statement a 'but'. Lamb Chop, dearest and best-beloved of all the moor ewes, has been a 'but' and an exception all her life. She and I have a relationship that is the summing-up of all that is best in the inter-relation of man and beast. We love one another.

She was bought at Hawes mart for fifty pence more years ago than I like to think about and spent her lambhood in a caravan, going for walks on a lead. She was given to me when her owner realised that her original intention of putting the dear soul in her mother's freezer was out of the question and she came to me when I was desperately searching for Swaledale gimmers to found a flock. Her adventures and escapades have been catalogued in my columns over the past few years and up on the moor are two ewes who owe their existence to the funny-looking little sheep with the grey face and silly horns who travels miles in answer to her name.

But this summer she proved her love and trust in a manner even I found hard to believe. She fell ill with a metabolic disease that wasted her to a doddery little skeleton, but she knew what must be done about it. She sat by the moor gate without moving for three days until I simply had to take notice; to ask her what was the matter. Any other Swaledale ewe would have wandered away up the moor to die. But Lamb Chop sat by the gate, calling out each time I passed by, until I had to investigate what I had looked upon as mere bloodymindedness. And when I realised I called the vet and he, despite my tardiness, saved the old sheep. Lamb Chop, in some strange way, is what it's all about and so, for the very last time, she has been made an exception. She did not go with the others to the hill sheep sale. She has been drafted down-country, but just by a field or two. She will winter in comfort with old Snuff.

I've arranged it – it's all going to happen. A very nice man is driving out all the way from Lancashire to fit a steel brace on old Snuff's teeth, before they get too loose and fall out. It's going to cost rather more than it would have done if he had been a local chap, and I had had a hundred ewes, but I don't mind – it's a drop in the ocean compared to what Snuff has earned for me over the years. I look on it as a present for an old friend.

She *is* rather old, as sheep go. And go they do, from around these parts when they get past their prime. I can accept this for most of my charges, being now in a position to sell out a few good, youngish ewes from the moor flock every year, to make room for the yearlings coming in, and it all works with the clockwork inevitability of the established practices of the countryside. But like Lamb Chop, Snuff is an exception.

She was never a moor sheep anyway – a Suffolk-cross lamb given by a farmer from when I had bought another lamb, as a sort of makeweight, she has been the mainstay of the smallholding since that first lucky day. She is, in fact 'Flock B' as far as the Ministry are concerned, and her records are stored in their offices along with those of the biggest flocks in the district. She has suffered and survived almost every disease in the shepherds' book, and is small, scruffy, blind in one eye, bandy-legged and cantankerous. She chases dogs. And life without her would be much the poorer.

In a financial sense, her lambs are an annual godsend, but in the more nebulous terms of the farmer small enough to afford a little sentiment, her woolly presence is a comfort in times of trouble and her friendship and trust are of inestimable value. She is one of the mainstays of the enterprise and to sell her, for any reason, would be unthinkable.

For quite a few years now, Sandra has asked me at regular

intervals when I'm going to 'send her in' and I've always
maintained that I'm not; not ever. If the time should come
when she can no longer look after her dear self, and I cannot
do it satisfactorily for her, then Our Beloved Vet, whom
God preserve, of Northallerton, can come and finish her
with dignity. I have always maintained that. But when I read
of the discovery of this method of splinting the teeth of an
older ewe, thus giving her many more years of useful life, I
decided that here, at last, was something I could do for my
old friend to repay all those years of faithful service. Something a little more practical than the packet of digestive
biscuits I always provide after the sale of her lambs!

But old Snuff has more friends than just the Drysdales.
Since I have written about her and she has appeared on TV
and her twin lambs featured in YTV's *It's a Vet's Life*, she
has gathered quite a number of fans, so the YTV Calendar
team are coming to film the fitting of her fine new teeth.
Lamb Chop, finally pensioned off from the moor, is going
to have a brace fitted, too, although I didn't quite know how
to react when Jim looked at the silly old sheep and said
lugubriously 'T'bugger'll live forever now'.

Both of them are to go to Jim's bluefaced Leicester tup as
soon as the job is done. The tup is already working his way
through the available talent with a will. But Snuff and Lamb
Chop were left behind when the others went off and
although Lamb Chop accepted this philosophically, old
Snuff was heartbroken. A couple of days later, her need
became pressing and she was forever wandering off to the
gate through which her companions had disappeared, calling dolefully.

I brought her home and fastened her up for a day and a
night. She mustn't be tupped before the teeth are fitted, as
the operation involves sitting her in a special cradle and
turning her through 180 degrees, a procedure which would
be dangerous to an in-lamb ewe; but she doesn't know, can't
understand, and I feel so sorry for her. If it could be granted

to me to talk to an animal just once, I think this would have to be the time, so that I could justify my hardheartedness to my dear Snuff. So that I could point out that she still has the annual event to look forward to, so that I could explain that, at least on this occasion, 'mother knows best'.

I have thought a lot about these ageing dependants, and about the wisdom of allowing myself, and the children, to become so attached to what must, if the farm is to make sense in business terms, be looked upon as transient assets. After all, the children are growing up now and the need to protect them from life's harsher realities is no longer so pressing. But we seem to have lost so much that is part of our beginnings. So much of that early hopefulness seems to have been mislaid along the way, set aside in the cause of expediency or common sense in the quest for the silk purse, that I have every intention of holding on to these special sows' ears to remind myself of the dream with which it all began. For myself, the greatest challenge of the future will be to remain true to those beginnings. The children must find their own challenges.

The boys are both at boarding school now. Only Nancy opted for the local comprehensive and takes an interest in the day-to-day running of the farm. Even now she has a late hatch of ducklings under her command, safe inside a cat-proof brooder I made her from two dressing-table drawers, hinged together.

The other night she and I sat together beside the ramshackle brooder, watching the ducklings play five-a-side football with a hard-boiled egg and laughing as they fell over themselves in their single-minded greed. The lamp shed a soft, golden light over everything and in its glow I noticed yet again that my daughter is growing into a very beautiful young woman. So much of the day-to-day care is over; so much is still to come.

Lost in thought, I didn't quite catch what it was Nancy was saying to me and she repeated it. 'I love the ducklings so much,' she was saying, 'I wish I could look after them always. I can't bear the thought of letting them go in the world among the cats and foxes. I wish there was a way to keep them little and fluffy forever.'

A little discouraged by my lack of response, she added 'Do you know what I mean, Mum?'

I did not look at her face, I stared hard at the new, feminine curves of the leg draped across mine, at the foot only a size less than my own in the smart, black shoe. 'Yes, love,' I said, softly, 'I know.'

Charity the jersey calf (author's photo)

Epilogue

All the long, cold winter Archie the guinea-fowl has sat on the perch in the carthouse and beside him there was always a space.

Dear Dodo, our first and best-loved guinea-fowl, died at Christmas and Archie was desolate. He couldn't bear to have her place taken by a mere hen and always bit any that were foolish enough to try to roost alongside him.

Last summer she had been kicked by a visiting pony and her leg broken. I splinted it for her and it mended, but she was never quite the same again. Archie was devoted to her all through her long convalescence and slowed down his own pace to match her dot-and-carry progress. Just as he shared the rearing of their young, so he shared the distress and handicap of the ugly little wife he had loved so long.

Loved, in fact, since it all began, and when poor Dodo finally died; slid quietly from her perch during one of the long winter nights, it was not only Archie who grieved for her. When I found him in the morning, talking quietly to the stiff little corpse that would no longer follow in his spindly footsteps, I cried for him, with him, because of him.

When I came to write the book that tells how we started our lives here, it both began and ended with Dodo and Archie. I can remember leaving a sort of safety-valve in the happy ending to their story, saying in print that I knew it could not last forever.

Nothing, no nothing, is forever. But when it happened, it hurt so, and telling myself that it must be far worse for poor Archie didn't take the grief away.

But spring came, as springs do. Archie's little police-helmet that grows like a wart on the top of his head lost its solitary droop. He smartened himself up and I thought often of getting him a new young wife. Only the memories held me back. Memories of how it used to be.

So much else seemed to have changed during that winter, and I mourned the loss of something I did not know I had until it had gone. My first book was published. My own face grinned back at me from the stationers' windows in town. Jim's hand had healed up; so had the place into which I had fitted. I was on the outside again.

For the first time in years I didn't feel well.

I lost the power to write; the will to create. All the gilt came off the gingerbread and it left a bitter taste. I suppose, among other things, it was a strain returning to normal after all the ballyhoo. What was really upsetting me was coming back to the life I loved and finding it had all changed, it wasn't the same any more. I can't put into words what has changed, but for a week or two I felt as Archie felt that cold, bleak morning.

Whatever it was that we both got up for, whatever it was that called us out into each new day was gone, gone and no amount of crying into the stillness of the morning could ever call it back again. And I cried often and woke lonely.

Last week our favourite dustman, axed from our round by an economising council, turned up with a carful of baby goats and a guinea-hen – for me and for Archie.

I stuffed the bird into the henhouse and shut the porthole. I was sure she'd fly away like old Archie did when I first let him out. But when I had settled the goat-babies with their friends and given them some food and a cuddle, I walked passed the henhut and saw that Archie was sitting on the step, talking low and earnestly to his new mate within. I let her out and she stepped straight into Dodo's place; you could almost hear the little click, like Lego bricks.

And it all swung back into gear. The pain came back again for a terrible moment. My own pain, my own grief – Archie's was gone and forgotten, drowned in quiet joy, and for a moment I hated the silly old bird for his fickleness, as Hamlet hated Gertrude.

But it didn't last long. How could I do other than share his joy at his new chance of another beginning. I suppose you can't have beginnings if you don't have ends. If you don't have ends, life is one long middle.

And when I made that remark to Nancy as we watched the silly pair parading on the roof, I realised with a start that it was my first attempt at a joke in weeks. A flurry of wings. A chunk of tile fell on my head. 'She's bombing us,' said Nancy. 'She must be an Argentinian guinea-fowl.'

And so we called her Evita. Archie and Evita – doesn't sound bad when you've said it a few times. 'Dodo and Archie' belongs to the precious past for which I have been grieving so sorely. And Archie and Evita is now, is tomorrow.

But not forever. Nothing is forever.

Pipsqueak at his adult best (author's photo)